NATIVE
AMERICAN
WEAPONS

NATIVE
AMERICAN
WEAPONS

Colin F. Taylor

University of Oklahoma Press
Norman

Credits

Editor: Charlotte Davies
Designer: John Heritage
Reproduction: Studio Technology
Printed in Spain

623.441

Acknowledgements

Many people have contributed in various ways to this project. In particular, I should mention the
late John C. Ewers, Senior Ethnologist at the Smithsonian Institution, Washington D.C. We both
discussed and examined several styles of North American Indian weaponry over the years, and the
fact that Dr. Ewers personally knew old-time Plains Indians who had been active caused him to
have special interest in intertribal warfare and the weapons used. Other friends – Gary Anderson,
Roland Bohr, Allen Chronister, Hugh Dempsey, Jim Hanson, Bill Holm, Robert Mucci, John
Painter, Dick Pohrt, Graeme Rimer of the Royal Armouries (London and Leeds), the late Russell
Robinson, William C. Sturtevant and Ian West – have all given an input in their own special way.
Thanks also to Charlotte Davies and John Heritage of Salamander Books Limited and, as always,
to my wife, Betty, for both editing and checking all the quotes and sources.

It is a pleasure to acknowledge that the final sections of this book were completed in the
tranquility of the home of Jody and Ned Martin in Hallack Creek Valley in northern California,
former heartland of the ingenious Miwok.

Additional captions: Page 2, The Shoshone warrior *Heebe-Tee-Tse* photographed circa 1900.
Page 3, A fine Bowie knife, this one has a horn handle and was said to have belonged to the
Hunkpapa Sioux leader, Sitting Bull.

Contents

Introduction

THIS VOLUME SURVEYS the variety of weaponry used by the North American Indians north of present-day Mexico from prehistoric times to the late nineteenth century, by which time various weapons introduced by Euro-Americans had largely replaced those of indigenous make.

These later weapons, such as the pipe tomahawk, knives, axes, arrow and spear heads, were generally based on native designs but replaced stone, bone, horn and hardened woods with iron and steel. When adopted, however, they were generally turned into something

Right: A Louisiana Indian war-party, one of whom is carefully covering their tracks. Stealth and surprise were characteristics of Native American warfare. Although the bows, quivers, clubs and hairstyles look stylized in this print, the use of guns and details of clan tattoos are accurate for the period.

Left: *Kutchin hunters and warriors, after a sketch by Alexander Hunter Murray at Fort Yukon, 1847-1848. Of Athapaskan stock, this powerful Subarctic tribe occupied the northern regions of Alaska and Yukon territory. The use of finely tanned caribou skin for clothing was typical of the period for this region. As shown here, it consisted of a distinctive shirt and pants decorated with dentalium shells and trade beads. The man on the left carries a trade gun in a protective skin case, powder horn and bullet pouch. The other man is armed with the more traditional bow and arrows – note the distinctive shape of the quiver.*

Left: *Weapons from the region of the Plains and Eastern Woodlands. The earliest weapon here is the ball-headed club (third from left), which possibly dates from 1700 and of Iroquois manufacture. The bows are typical of the Plains region for the mid-nineteenth century. About 40 inches (1m) in length, the bow on the far left is partially covered with snake skin; the one on the far right is sinew-backed. The stone-headed club (lower left) is an Apache "slingshot" type which contrasts with the conical stone-headed club (right) from the Central Plains region. In the middle is a trade pipe tomahawk (probably from the Crow) and adjacent to it is a so-called Missouri war axe.*

very **Indian** by use of various embellishments, such as engraving, carving or the addition of paint, quillwork and beads (p. 8).

Classification has been according to five broad categories relating to function – striking, cutting, piercing, defensive and symbolic; these form the five main chapters in the volume. The use of pre-contact copper and the later magnificent impact of trade iron and the horse on weapon styles is dealt with in Chapters II, III and IV.

The subject is vast; a focus on one cultural area alone, even one tribe, could produce a substantial study and so this volume must be viewed as a broad overview of a fascinating, but very extensive, topic. Some techniques of fabrication have been described. This includes the widespread war club which had a stone head held in place by rawhide which also covered the handle and which was generally sheathed in soft buckskin. Depending on the region and period, the club was then quilled or beaded (p. 8 lower left). The main emphasis, however, has been on the finished weapon. The footnotes refer to further sources.

Detailed attention has been given to the pipe tomahawk, the early history of which is still quite obscure; some early pictorial evidence has suggested that the original idea of a combined weapon and pipe may have come from the American Indians themselves (p. 29) rather than, as has generally been contended, invented by Euro-Americans. The various styles of pipe tomahawk have been referred to as 'English', 'Spanish' and 'French". However, as one student of the tomahawk has observed, a large number were probably fabricated by local blacksmiths rather than wholesale production in Europe.[1]

The early types of war clubs used in eastern North America, are covered in Chapter I and looked at in some depth since such weapons were often the precursors to those which were refined and enhanced by Euro-Americans. These include the anciently used clubs of a 'pickaxe' type, now to be found in the National Museums of Denmark and Sweden and dating from the mid-seventeenth century. Possibly of Nanticoke or Delaware make, these probably had a wider distribution than is generally recognized, as did sword-shaped and ballheaded clubs. Early forms of weapons made for the Indian trade were often inspired by these various styles but replaced with iron, steel and sometimes brass – a recurring theme which was generally readily accepted by the indigenous peoples.

Above: His-oo-san-ches *or 'Little Spaniard', a Comanche warrior in an engraving after George Catlin who visited the tribe in 1834. The warrior is armed with a bow, lance and shield of typical styles for the Southern Plains at this time.*

Less so was one style of defensive weapon on the Plains. Here, attempts by traders to introduce **metal** shields, and replace those of rawhide, were opposed by Blackfeet holy men who contended that the **designs** on the shields gave far more spiritual protective power than the simple mechanical protection afforded by a disc of heavy metal. Obviously, religious and military symbolism, as well as tribal economics, entered the equation.

The section on piercing weapons (Chapter III) looks at the use of the atlatl, or spearthrower, which pre-dated the use of the bow in North America by thousands of years. When the atlatl was first encountered by the Spanish under De Soto, its frightening effectiveness against mail-armored soldiers – due to a three to five times energy increase imparted to the projectile – filled the Spaniards with consternation. Little wonder, as is discussed in the main text, the spearthrower continued in use, particularly amongst the Inuit. Not only was it a highly effective killing weapon but when used, it only required one hand.

Chapter IV describes defensive weapons. Here, the use of body armor is considered, together with warrior and horse shields, warfare tactics and village fortifications. All were later modified with the introduction of steel weapons and the gun. Protective symbols then dominated rather than actual mechanical protection – the subject of Chapter V.

The ingenuity of North American Indian weaponry is documented and recognized; how, over thousands of years, it was developed and ingeniously matched the environment where it was used. It was highly functional, often decorative and proudly carried in war and parade.

There is, perhaps, a slight bias to Plains Indian weapons and warfare. This is because collections and data are particularly rich for this area and it is also more recent in the Indian-White confrontation. The use of such weapons, however, was clearly embedded in ancient styles and history when ancestors of the historic Plains tribes lived in the Arctic, the northern boreal forests, the woodlands to the east and, perhaps, even south into Mexico.

Below: *Pawnee warriors and their interpreter, circa 1868. The men are stripped to the waist and wear little restrictive clothing or accoutrements – typical of Pawnee warriors about to enter battle.*

CHAPTER ONE

Striking Weapons

"Pemakiwoto"
(Lakota for 'strike and hurt/kill')

A VARIETY OF STRIKING weapons were used throughout ancient North America, most of which were designated for warfare. As will be discussed, however, a number were relegated to ceremonial use or employed solely for special functions.

Whilst most of these weapons could be classified as hatchets or clubs – the term "war club" particularly was widely used – others such as the tomahawk tended to fall into a class of their own. This

Right: *Three stone club heads: the one on the left is probably made of chert, the two on the right of flint. These have been grooved for attachment to a wooden handle. The resultant clubs could be formidable weapons and of a type widely used for thousands of years in North America.*

was certainly true by the mid-eighteenth century. With the passage of time, the term "tomahawk" referred to a weapon largely fabricated by whites and having a metal blade.[1]

Ancient stone clubs in North America

Early clubs of indigenous manufacture often display exceptional skills in stone- and flint-working. For example, those from the Southeast and found in the ancient mounds of Tennessee and Alabama are invariably monolithic, with both the handle and blade carved from a single piece of stone (above). Generally about a foot (30cm) or more in length, many were made of a green stone with superb native lapidarian work. Whilst undoubtedly formidable weapons, it has been speculated that some of the finest may have also served as maces or were used in a ceremonial context. The perforated knob extending from the end of the handle (above) suggests the use of a wrist thong, reinforcing the contention of possible employment in ritual or dance. Although not exclusive to the Southeast (large

Above: *A ceremonial war mace made from jasper, a flint-like material. This particular specimen was found in Mound Spiro in the Ohio Valley.*

Right and inset: *A magnificent early style wooden club which was generally referred to by the early colonists in Virginia as a tomahawk. It is made of a single piece of wood and displays a sharp drop to the ballhead which is a typical feature of such clubs. At times the heads were elaborately carved, as in this presentation piece.*

monolithic clubs have been described for Northwest Coast tribes such as the Tlingit), they seem to have reached their highest development in this area. This may be due to the influence of early contact with tribes on the islands of the West Indies where such monolithic clubs were far more prevalent. Associated weaponry was made of chipped flint or jasper, some of the finest being found in the Spiro Mounds of present-day Ohio. Dating from prehistoric times, these weapons were shaped with great skill (p. 13) – razor-sharp, they could decapitate an enemy at a single blow. Masterpieces of the chipping art, some of the finest examples were obviously carried by distinguished individuals – song leaders, shamans, chiefs – but the style shows that the skills were available to make weapons for everyday use.

The stone-headed club

Of wider distribution were those clubs with stone heads generally set at the end of a wooden handle. Typical stone heads – two of which are shown on the right on p. 12 – were found on the banks of the Vermillion River in present-day eastern South Dakota. They are of a type commonly used by the prehistoric pedestrian Plains warriors

Right: *A rendering of the formation and equipment of* Outina, *a Timucua (Florida) war chief (Feest, 1988: 35). Note the heavy oval-headed (wooden?) clubs carried by most of the warriors; an unusual style for eastern North America.*

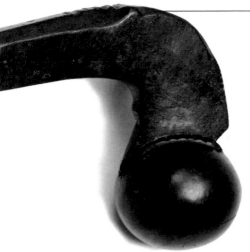

and later by equestrian nomads who peopled the Plains from about 1750 onwards. The stone head was attached to the handle by shaving thin the upper end of the wooden shaft and then bending it around the groove which had been made in the stone; the pared wood was then lashed into place with rawhide thongs. Alternatively, a broad band of rawhide secured the head to the shaft, which might be inserted into a hole drilled in the stone. The rawhide was generally softened by first soaking it in water and then tightly bound; when it dried, the subsequent shrinkage held the head securely in place. This technique is evident on the club shown on p. 17 (right) and the handle, as was common with this style, has been covered with rawhide; additionally, it has been decorated with both beads and porcupine quills.

An alternative, related style of stone-headed club was a heavy round-headed stone entirely covered with rawhide or heavy buckskin, which was in turn sewn around the wooden handle. It left 2 inches (5cm) or so of rawhide between the end of the handle and the stone head free. When used in combat, the relatively free-moving head dealt a lethal blow. Such weapons were not uncommon on the Plains, in the Southwest and on the Plateau. It has been suggested that they originated west of the Rocky Mountains, whilst its eastern limits "were the Great Lakes where it was observed among the Menomini."[2]

Wooden clubs

Many early clubs of indigenous manufacture were of a simple knob-stick variety (p. 17, left, and p. 19). Typical were those used by the Pima and Yuman tribes in the Southwest and made of a hard wood; mesquite was the most popular. The natural shape was carved to produce a very formidable weapon in the hands of a resolute man, whose technique of combat was to invariably employ a powerful upward movement in an attempt to break or crush the jaw of an opponent.

Above: *The Mohawk leader,* Etow oh Koam, *whose portrait was painted in London in 1710. He is carrying a finely carved ballheaded club which from earliest times was much favored by the Iroquois and other Woodland tribes.*

Far more elaborate wooden clubs were developed by the Northwest Coast tribes, such as the Nootka and Kwakiutl. Exhibiting carvings which not infrequently made reference to tribal mythology, such clubs were more used in the ceremonial context rather than on the battlefield and some were referred to as "slave killers" (although there is little evidence to suggest that they actually performed that function).

For everyday use – in both hunting and warfare – clubs were often spatula-shaped and made of either hard wood or carved whalebone, which was generally sharpened along the edge and sometimes embellished with carvings on the blade and handle.[3] These clubs were simi-

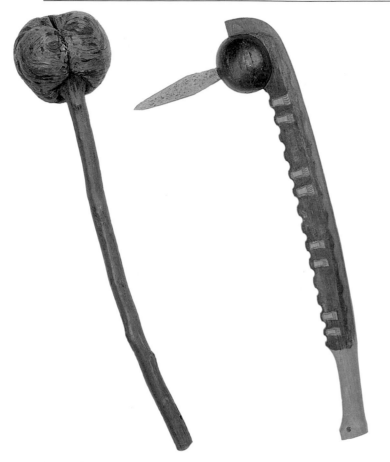

Far left: *A ballheaded wooden club collected in 1838 from the Karankawa Indians of Texas. Some 25 inches (62cm) in length, the head is shaped from a tree burl.* **Near left:** *A Yankton Sioux club dating from the 1870s; structurally, it is a style which clearly had its origins in the Eastern Woodlands.*

Above: *A short-handled stoned-headed club dating from circa 1860 and probably Sioux. The naturally shaped stone-head, probably of agate, is attached to a rawhide-covered wooden handle. The band around the head is decorated with porcupine quills and the handle partially wrapped with blue and white seed beads.*

lar in shape – although smaller – to the paddles used by the Northwest Coast tribes. The paddles shown on p. 20 were collected from the Tlingit in the 1870s. Traveling in elaborately carved and painted canoes (p. 21), war-parties often beat time on the gunwale during confrontation and the pointed paddles (generally made of yew or maple wood and polished smooth with sharkskin) might then be utilized as makeshift – although formidable – offensive weapons.[4] An unusual type of carved club collected from the Kiowa is shown on p. 19. Heavily embossed with metal tacks and painted red and green, the distinctive notched shape seems to have had early and wide dis-

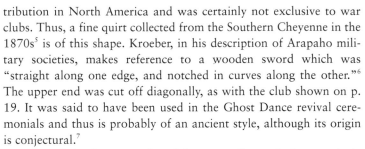

Below: *War clubs collected from the Pima of the Gila River region in present-day Arizona. Made from a mesquite wood, which is particularly hard, they differ considerably from those clubs used by the Woodland and Plains tribes and are closer to those developed by the powerful Yuma to their north; they used this 'potato-masher'-type club in their closequarter hand-to-hand fighting.*

tribution in North America and was certainly not exclusive to war clubs. Thus, a fine quirt collected from the Southern Cheyenne in the 1870s[5] is of this shape. Kroeber, in his description of Arapaho military societies, makes reference to a wooden sword which was "straight along one edge, and notched in curves along the other."[6] The upper end was cut off diagonally, as with the club shown on p. 19. It was said to have been used in the Ghost Dance revival ceremonials and thus is probably of an ancient style, although its origin is conjectural.[7]

Some of the finest wooden clubs, generally made from a single piece of wood and obviously of considerable antiquity, are those from the Eastern Woodlands.

Styles of war clubs in eastern North America

Brasser's (1961) detailed analysis of the clubs used in eastern North America identifies four main types which, prior to the forced movement of several tribes west under the pressure of white settlers, were used mainly east of the Mississippi River. Usually made from wood, he refers to them as the pick axe, sword, gun-shaped and ballhead types.

Pick axe styles were described as early as 1540 by the Spanish explorer, De Soto, who visited groups on the Savannah. They were provided with copper or stone blades or celts. Such celts had a sharp edge on one side and a diamond-shaped point at the back; a variant was that used in the Virginia region which had a horn or stone celt which was pointed at both ends, the celt itself being driven through the wooden handle. Its use as a weapon, carried in the left hand with shield on the right arm, was illustrated by the French explorer, Samuel de Champlain, who travelled to the Iroquois on the Hudson and Mohawk Rivers in 1609.[8] (See Chapter IV, p. 82 for an early engraving of this illustration.)

A variant of this style of club was the use of a rawhide cord or strap which attached the celt to the handle. As Brasser has observed, it suggests a possible relationship to the hammer-type club so popular further west and described earlier (p. 17).

Two examples of the pick axe-type club are represented in the collections of the National Museums of Denmark and Sweden.

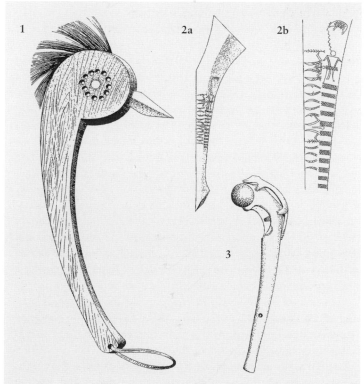

Above: *A wooden club collected in the early 1900s from the Kiowa by the ethnologist, James Mooney. Such clubs resemble some types of quirts or whips, particularly popular on the Southern Plains.*

Left: *Early styles of wooden clubs: (1) Osage which gives the impression of the head of a bird. (2a and 2b) Sauk, circa 1760 gun-shaped type. Detail of engravings possibly war tally marks. (3) Early Iroquoian-type ballheaded club, probably early eighteenth century.*

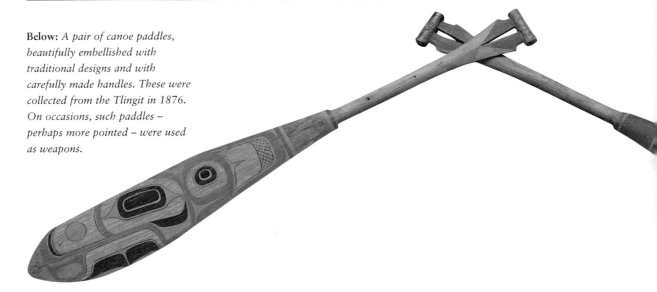

Below: *A pair of canoe paddles, beautifully embellished with traditional designs and with carefully made handles. These were collected from the Tlingit in 1876. On occasions, such paddles – perhaps more pointed – were used as weapons.*

Described as "unique pieces"[9] and dating from before 1650,[10] it is probable that they were acquired in the region of the lower Delaware River where a small Swedish colony had been founded in about 1650.[11]

The efficiency of these clubs as striking weapons has been questioned, particularly because of the weak attachment of the blade to the haft.[12] Nevertheless, these rare specimens probably represent a style which had relatively wide distribution – they were used not only by the Iroquois, but also by such tribes as the Nanticoke, Delaware and Susquehannocks to their south and east, and perhaps even to tribes beyond.[13]

A club compared by early observers to a scimitar but more recently referred to as a "sword-type"[14] seems to have had its origins in the south. Indeed, a weapon used by the Aztecs strongly resembled the sword-club and it was a style widely used early on in the Southeast by tribes of the Florida Keys, the Muskogeans and Powhatans. Varying considerably in style[15] – some had shark teeth or flints set along the edge, others were notched or plain – the sword-club was later popular amongst the Iroquois and extended as far north as the tribes of southern New England. A relatively simple form of this club was col-

Right: *A rendering of Haida canoes as they may have appeared in warfare, circa 1870. Such canoes were made from a single hollowed-out tree trunk by skilful use of adze and chisel as well as controlled burning. Designs such as the Thunderbird made reference to the victor of the heavens, whilst that of the killerwhale leant toward the spirit and Lord who dominated the underworld powers, which gave confidence to Haida war-parties.*

lected from the Tuscarora by Prince Maximilian du Wied. Some 2 feet (62cm) in length, it had been preserved and used by the Tuscarora in their dances, "as a memory to their past."[16] Although at the time of Maximilian's visit the Tuscarora had long been associated with the Iroquois, their earlier homeland was considerably further south, perhaps extending as far as the coast of the present-day North Carolina.

The utilization of a sword-shaped club as a symbol of the past certainly suggests that this was an important style of weapon in the Southeast – a contention supported by Brasser's 1961 research.[17] The shape, with distinctive notched edges, was used in the fabrication of the quirts used by some western tribes (alluded to earlier on p. 18). It is therefore possible that this style of quirt derived from an ancient and popular sword-like weapon, memories of which were brought west by displaced tribes, particularly those from the Southeast such as the Delaware, Creek, Seminole and Cherokee.[18]

Most impressive of all Eastern Woodland striking weapons are the

Below: Waatopenot, *"The Eagle's Bill", a Chippewa chief, painted by James Otto Lewis at the Fond du Lac council in 1826. This man is carrying a classic gunstock-shaped war club which is embellished with brass-headed studs. The basic club style is ancient.*

magnificent ballheaded clubs (pp. 14–15) much favored by the Iroquois and Huron and described as early as 1635. One notable authority on the Iroquois described such clubs as "a heavy weapon two feet [62cm] in length made of ironwood with a globular head five or six inches in diameter (p. 16). The head sometimes resembled a human face or a ball enclosed by claws."[19] A fine example of this style of club is now in the collection of the National Museum of Scotland (pp. 14–15), although it dates from circa 1850, and thus was probably a presentation piece rather than a functional weapon. It reflects the very high degree of skill used by the Iroquois (and other tribes) in the carving of naturalistic effigies and at the same time it "also displays an assemblage of symbolic materials and paint that has often disappeared from similar pieces collected during the early contact period."[20] Whilst tree roots or tree knots were said to be used in the fabrication of such clubs[21], one favored source was apparently a sapling which grew from the sides of a river bank and which curved upward toward the light; clubs made of such wood were obviously of great strength and elasticity.[22]

Although not a feature exclusive to the ballheaded club, a number of the early examples exhibit a series of engraved motifs, such as stylized depictions of a horned serpent, underwater panthers, Thunderbirds and human figures. In addition, there are bands and crosses which may be indicative of tally marks – perhaps coups counted, prisoners

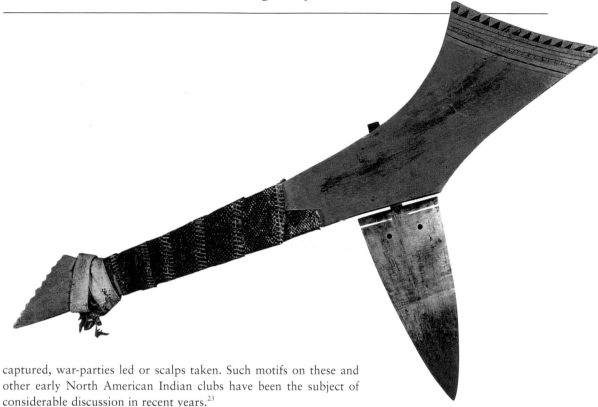

captured, war-parties led or scalps taken. Such motifs on these and other early North American Indian clubs have been the subject of considerable discussion in recent years.[23]

Gunstock clubs – so called because they were carved in the form of a European gunstock – were popular and widely used in the Woodland area, Peterson recording that they were in use as early as "the beginning of the 17th century."[24] Generally some 30 inches (75 cm) or more in length, they usually differed from the earlier style of sword-type club by having a blade of flint, horn or iron set into the upper end (pp. 22–23); the stock itself was often decorated with engravings or brass-headed trade tacks. This style of club continued in popularity in the Midwest amongst such tribes as the Sauk and Fox as well as the Eastern Sioux. A particularly fine example, collected by Duke Paul of Württemberg in the 1820s and probably from the Osage, is shown in on p. 23; the spear-point-type steel blade used here was a very popular trade item.

By the 1850s, such clubs were to be found amongst the Lakota on

Above: *A magnificent gunstock-shaped club collected in the 1820s by the traveler, Duke Paul of Württemberg. These clubs were particularly popular at this time with both Eastern Woodland and the semisedentary tribes of the Middle-Missouri region. This one, probably from the Osage, has a trade steel blade and a handle wrapped with snakeskin.*

the western Plains, although the stock itself was generally slimmer and longer than those formerly used by the more eastern tribes.[25] A variant on this style of club was one which had two or more steel knife blades set in the edge (p. 35). A particularly dangerous weapon at close quarters in the hands of a resolute man, such styles were popular in the period 1860–1880; one was collected from the Hunkpapa Sioux leader, Sitting Bull, by General Nelson A. Miles and is now in the National Museum of the American Indian, Washington DC.[26]

The so-called "Missouri war hatchet" was found in use by Lewis and Clark when they stayed with the Mandan on the middle Missouri River (in present-day North Dakota) in the winter of 1805–1806. Meriwether Lewis was particularly interested in this style of weapon since, in his opinion, it was a "battle-ax, of a very inconvenient figure." Such axes, he said, were fabricated of iron, the blade being "extremely thin and from seven to nine inches long... the eye... is circular and about an inch in diameter... the handle is straight, and 12 or 15 inches long; the whole weighs about a pound."[27] The combination of the blade to handle length rendered such a weapon, in Lewis' opinion, "of very little strength, particularly as it is always used on horseback."[28] Nevertheless, it would appear that the Mandan, as well as at least nine other tribes in the region, favored this weapon, which seems to have been introduced by French traders some time in the 1700s. The expedition's blacksmith was kept busy making such axes, mainly in exchange for corn, which helped the expedition to survive the brutal winter when temperatures often plunged almost to 50° below zero. Being without a steel edge, of thin iron and often having decorative piercings in the form of a "bleeding heart," the Missouri

Above: *The Fox chief,* Nesouaquoit, *"Bear in the forks of a tree", painted in Washington in 1837. This man carries a classic Missouri war hatchet; the decorated blade is of an unusually large size.*

24

war hatchet, it might appear to white observers, was more for cere-monial use than for use in actual warfare. However, as Peterson observes, this may be "an excellent illustration of the fact that European standards may not always be used in judging the use an Indian may have had for an object."[29] The Missouri war axe continued to be used by the Missouri River tribes as late as the mid-nineteenth cen-tury.[30] Thus, the artist/explorer Rudolph Kurz sketched an Omaha carrying such a weapon in the vicinity of Bellevue, Nebraska, in

Below: *Battle between a Cheyenne and the Mandan chief, Mato-tope, "Four Bears", as depicted by Four Bears in 1834. This was a particularly dramatic battle. Note the use of the Missouri war axe by the victorious Mandan chief, who himself was badly injured.*

1851.[31] Perhaps at this time, however, they were considered more for ceremonial use and indeed it has been observed they were handed down as heirlooms "in even more recent times"; the height of its popularity, however, seems to have been "between 1810 and 1830."[32]

Also reported in use amongst the Mandan was the so-called "spontoon tomahawk". Even as early as 1805, though, it was considered an old-fashioned weapon and even more inconvenient than the Missouri war hatchet. The large blade was invariably fashioned from one piece of wrought iron which was bent round at the top to form the eye, welded on to the blade. Two sections were then cut from the body of the blade and bent outward; further decorative features were holes drilled near the top. The length of such blades could be up to 15 inches (38cm), although the shape has been likened in appearance to large door hinges. The inspiration for this form of war axe probably derives from the espontoon, a polearm which was commonly carried by commissioned officers in the 1700s. The espontoon, in turn, derived from the partizan, an officer's spear which was commonly used in the sixteenth and seventeenth centuries. Little wonder that even as early as 1805, Lewis and Clark described them as the "older fassion"![33] The spontoon tomahawk has been described with some justification as the French type (of tomahawk), resembling the fleur-de-lis;[34] further, the earliest specimens come from areas traditionally associated with the French in North America – the St. Lawrence Valley, Great Lakes, Lake Champlain and extending down to the mouth of the Mississippi. Such tomahawks, however, were not exclusively made by the French. Certainly after 1763, when the British took over the region formerly occupied by the French, they were probably produced by not only the British but by Americans and Canadians, mainly for the lucrative fur trade.[35] By the mid-nineteenth century, the spontoon tomahawk (with several variations) was widely distributed, extending across the Prairies and

Above: *A Crow warrior with a spontoon-type tomahawk which was often referred to as the "French type". These weapons date back to the early eighteenth century, although the style was still popular with the Crow well into the twentieth century,. They were generally – as shown here – much elaborated. (Painting by Bill Holm).*

Far left: *The Shoshone, Heebe-Tee-Tse, photographed circa 1900. Shown here is a modified form of Missouri war axe – a triangular section is cut out of the blade, which is probably of pewter.*

Above: *A fine steel pipe tomahawk (1860–1880) where the classical features of the Plains Indian style have been embellished with a detailed pictographic-type warrior on horseback and enemy prostrate on the ground (right, detail). The handle has been file-branded and additionally decorated with brass tacks.*

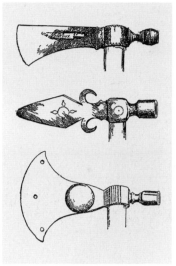

Plains to the Plateau region. It found particular favour with the Crow and their friends, the Nez Perce, from about 1870 onwards. Steel was only seldom used in their fabrication; however, as Peterson has observed, the iron blade would "inflict a serious wound in combat" and also that "later specimens seem to have been primarily ceremonial in use."[36]

A question of terminology
References to "tomahawk", as against "club" or "hatchet", in the discussion of the spontoon blade raises several points with regard to the nomenclature used to describe North American Indian striking

Above: *Styles of pipe tomahawk contrasted. (Top) Early style of axe-like tomahawk, circa 1800. (Middle) A spontoon tomahawk. Some of the earliest specimens (circa 1750) suggest French influence. (Bottom) Flaring blade tomahawk resembling those widely used in Europe. This type may be Spanish-influenced.*

Above left: *The Seneca chief, "Cornplanter", painted by Frederic Bartoli in 1796. This is one of the few renderings of an early style of pipe tomahawk where a clay pipe appears to have been inserted at the front of the handle (in combination with a spiked hatchet).*

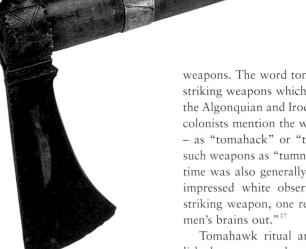

Above: *An iron pipe tomahawk, fitted with a beechwood handle, embellished with silver. This is a particularly elaborate piece, being engraved and also inlaid with an image of a bowie knife. Probably of English make, it was collected in West Virginia, circa 1873, but undoubtedly dates to the early nineteenth century.*

weapons. The word tomahawk was originally applied to a group of striking weapons which were commonly and anciently used by both the Algonquian and Iroquoian tribes of eastern North America. Early colonists mention the word from this region – with slight variations – as "tomahack" or "tommahick", whilst the Mahican referred to such weapons as "tumnahecan". The wooden ballheaded club at this time was also generally referred to as a "tomahawk" and it clearly impressed white observers with its effectiveness; as an offensive striking weapon, one recorded that it was heavy enough "to knock men's brains out."[37]

Tomahawk ritual and symbolism was undoubtedly well established at a very early period. Thus, it is recorded that when council was called to deliberate war, a tomahawk, entirely painted red, was placed on the ground by the chief. If the council agreed that a war-party should be initiated, the young war-chief leader raised the tomahawk, dancing and singing war songs. This was a pattern not exclusive to eastern tribes; with some variations, but basically similar, it was replicated in a number of other regions, particularly on the Plains.

With the passage of time and with a wide variety of striking weapons to describe, in modern anthropological parlance the word "tomahawk" "tends to restrict the term to metal axes."[38] The term "pipe tomahawk" almost exclusively refers to a combination of a pipe and weapon, made of metal, although at times there are some interesting combinations of other materials One example is the weapon carried by the Seneca chief, "Cornplanter" in the fascinating portrait produced in 1796 (p. 29)[39] – the blade is made of metal but the bowl appears to be clay.

The pipe tomahawk

Perhaps of all the various tools and weapons on offer from the European (and later American and Canadian) market to the North American Indian during the lucrative years of the fur trade (circa 1650–1870) nothing was more appealing than – as the English put it – the "smoak tomahawk". Although the term covers an immense number of styles, the basic construction combined both pipe and war hatchet in one single unit – symbols of both peace and war. It was a highly prized and exceptionally useful implement. As was observed of the Cherokee who had adopted the pipe tomahawk as early as the 1750s, "this is one of their most useful pieces of field-furniture, serving all the offices of hatchet, pipe, and sword."[40]

The history of the pipe tomahawk extends back to at least the first half of the eighteenth century, possibly as early as 1709–1710, since a portrait of one of the Iroquois "Kings" who visited London at this time depicts a metal hatchet with a flaring blade. At the top it appears that a pipe-bowl is attached, although it could simply be the opposing spike or hook of the halberd-type tomahawk.

Such weapons were named after an English polearm weapon developed in the late fourteenth century and modified by at least the early 1700s into the "battle axe" tomahawk for the North American Indian trade.[41] Whatever the precise date of invention, by the middle of the eighteenth century, pipe tomahawks were commonly used, although they were at least four times more expensive than the relatively simple war hatchet. Those inletted with steel or combined with brass seem to have been valued at almost twice that amount.[42]

Who first invented the pipe tomahawk, is conjectural. In an insightful discussion, the scholar Richard Pohrt, who has made a spe-

Above: *A spontoon type pipe tomahawk of a style which dates to the mid-nineteenth century, and is possibly Sauk or Fox. The specimen has an unusual flat strap.*

Above left: *The head of a pipe tomahawk, probably Santee Sioux. This has been carved from catlinite, a soft red stone quarried in present-day Minnesota.*

Above right: *A fine steel pipe tomahawk with pierced blade and bowl made from a gun barrel. Probably Hunkpapa Sioux, circa 1870.*

Right: The Yankton Sioux, "Flying Pipe" in full regalia, photographed circa 1870. He wears a quilled shirt, fringed with hair-locks and dentalium shell necklace and ear ornaments. In his right hand is a spontoon-type pipe tomahawk, which was popular with some of the Sioux at this time.

cial study of the tomahawk, concluded that the possibility that it was the brain-child of a North American Indian could not be discounted. Pohrt refers to the fact that in 1779-80, David Zeisberger, a Moravian missionary, reported that Indians in present-day Ohio were well acquainted with blacksmithing and fashioned metal hatchets and axes "right well". Additionally, it is noted the most commonly used material for pipe-stems was ash sapling, which was the same material used for the handles of pipe tomahawks. Pohrt concludes, "It seems but a short step for an Indian, patiently fitting a handle in a hatchet head, to realize that he had the makings of a pipe stem. The addition of a pipe bowl to the poll, or back, of his hatchet blade would produce a dual purpose object – one that could be used for chopping or smoking."[43]

The use of ash for the handle not only gave a stronger wooden stem which could take high polish, but also enabled a hole to be com-

Below: *Pictograph of a Cheyenne warrior wearing a warshirt embellished with ermine fringes. He is striking a U.S. soldier with a Warrior Society membership lance. This may be more than just a symbolic coup count, as the lance appears to be pointed. Collected by the traveler, William Blackmore, from Two Lance's camp on the Platte River in 1874.*

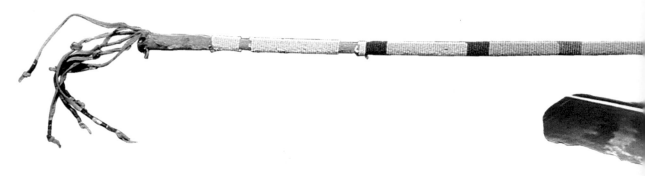

Above: A beaded coup stick of a widely distributed type, used by several tribes on the Central and Northern Plains. This one may well be Assiniboin, dating from circa 1870. Striking an enemy – counting coup – with a relatively harmless stick such as this was regarded as a war honor of the highest grade.

paratively easily bored through for use in smoking. Ash has a soft pith center which is easily removed by burning or splitting the wood lengthwise, cutting out the pith and then sticking the two pieces back together. The handle was often decorated with heavy brass-headed trade tacks and the lower end covered with buckskin to facilitate a firm grip. An extension of the end cover was, particularly on dress occasion tomahawks, elaborately quilled or beaded – the particular technique of embellishment (type of bead, patterns and color) was indicative of tribal origin.

Although early Hudson Bay trade lists tabulate various types of hatchets and axes on offer to Indians in the fur trade, there is little evidence to suggest that the pipe tomahawk itself was manufactured on a large scale in Europe.[44] The majority seem to have been made by rural blacksmiths and exhibit an enormous variety of design. The inspiration for some of these designs undoubtedly derived from early English, French and possibly Spanish weaponry. However, as Pohrt has observed, "Most tomahawks show a great variety in design, size, and decorative detail, and lack the standardization usually associated with quantity production."[45] In addition, Pohrt found, after extensive examination of tomahawks over a period of more than thirty years, that it was very rare for a pipe tomahawk to be stamped with a trade mark or the maker's name, which was common practice with English (and other) manufacturers of metal weapons and tools. It seems that the pipe tomahawk, invented by either an Indian or an Englishman, was a unique, highly prized item, largely produced by skilled American artisans.[46]

Right: *Spotted Eagle, a Miniconjou Sioux, photographed by L. A. Huffman in the 1880s. He wears a distinctive quilled shirt and has armbands of grizzly bear claws. Of particular interest, however, is the long, slender gunstock club with three knife blades set in the upper edge. These clubs were particularly favored by the Plains Sioux from about 1860 onwards.*

CHAPTER TWO

Cutting Weapons

"They raised a knife in the right hand and pointed towards heaven saying 'I have stated the truth'"
(Oath-taking of the Plains tribes. Lewis Henry Morgan, 1860)

Below: *Chipped flint and chert were used for a variety of sharp-edged tools. This Folsom blade is of a style used 11,000 years ago in the region of present-day Northeast Colorado. The fluting is a distinguishing characteristic of such points.*

FROM TIME IMMEMORIAL, cutting weapons of various styles have been used throughout North America. Many, of course, were used as tools and utensils whilst others were specifically designed for warfare. Essential for survival was the need to scrape, saw, bore and cut various materials and naturally, the type of tool for these processes varied considerably; not only in shape and size, but also in the choice of material for the cutting edge.

In general, scrapers – a tool of very wide distribution in North America – resembled a chisel blade, invariably with a beveled edge and made of a siliceous stone such as chert, jasper, agate or basanite.

The simplest scrapers were held in the hand, generally with some padding, whilst more elaborate versions were set into handles of wood, bone or horn. Those used for tanning hides or shaping wood were particularly well developed in several cultural areas, such as on the Great Plains and Northwest Coast, where hide-tanning and wood-carving reached a very high degree of perfection.

The same was true of both sawing and boring tools, the former with a serrated edge, the latter a sharp pointed edge, and either held directly in the hand or provided with a haft so that the boring could be achieved generally by vibration or rotation. Relatively soft stone such as argillite or catlinite[1] could be shaped and perforated with some ease, as could various woods, bone and horn. In the hands of

a skilled artisan, ancient – mainly stone – tools largely satisfied the needs of the North American Indian, although even this comparatively sophisticated stone-age technology obviously had its limitations; flint tools often broke or were easily blunted and remaking or sharpening them was a lengthy process.

The production of knives particularly tested the skill of the maker, great ingenuity being displayed in both selection of suitable material and in the shaping of the blade. Whilst virtually every material capable of taking an edge was used – such as teeth, bone, horn, shell, wood and, on occasions, native copper and possibly meteoric iron – it was stone, as with the scraping, sawing and boring tools described earlier, which was predominately the favored material.

The technique of flaking was an essential, skilled process to be used in the production of a sharp-edged knife or dagger. Here, the natural edges or forms of the stone[2] were modified by fracturing with a specially made flaking tool. The "flaker", as it was commonly called, had a blade generally of antler, ivory or hard bone, set in a wooden handle. This was applied to the stone edge and, with a quick movement (at the same time exerting a strong pressure), a flake of the stone was forced off. A skilled individual worked rapidly, moving along the outline of the blade, producing a razor-sharp, although fragile, cutting edge.

Not only were such knives of great practical value in both the

Above: Sharp-edged obsidian blades were a particular specialty of a number of the Californian tribes. The Hupa, for example, carried beautifully worked red or black obsidian blades of this type in their ceremonials. Highly valued, they were a symbol of both wealth and status, as well as a demonstration of a highly skilled stone-working technology.

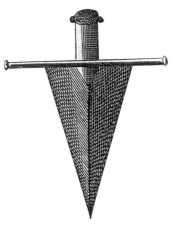

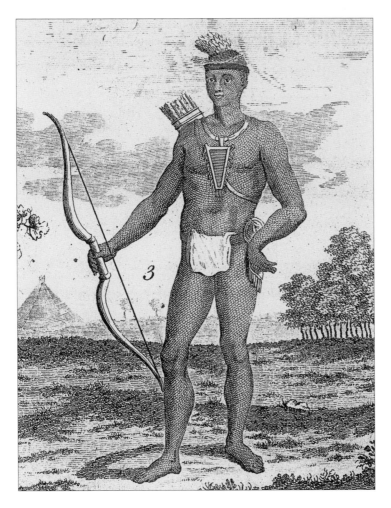

3

Above and left: *A chief of the Naudowessie (Santee Sioux) after descriptions by the traveler, Jonathan Carver, who traveled to the region of present-day Minnesota in 1766–1767. The distinctive knife (above) worn at the neck, was described as a symbol of high rank amongst the Sioux – a concept which prevailed well into the nineteenth century.*

Right: *A warrior of the "Chippeways easterly of the Mississippi" after Jonathan Carver (circa 1766). More detailed than that of the Sioux shown left – note leggings, moccasins, gun and tomahawk – the custom of wearing the knife in a decorated sheath at the throat, as for the Sioux, is also documented here.*

hunt and war, but there was also considerable ceremony and symbolism associated with a number of them. In California, for example, ceremonial knife blades 20 inches (50cm) or more in length and some 2½ inches (6cm) broad at the widest part were carried in ceremonials such as the Hupa White Deerskin Dance.[3] They were generally made of chipped obsidion and commonly wrapped with a buckskin

handle to prevent cutting the hands; large ones, it is said, "can not be purchased at any price."[4]

One recent scholar has observed that the ancient stone knives and blades – some dating back to at least 12,000 B.C. – were "flint art-form masterpieces... [which] are a tribute to the skills of the earliest American [Indian] knife maker."[5]

The use of copper

Although various types of stone were used very early on by the indigenous Americans, it is recorded that some time before the arrival of Europeans to the region of the Great Lakes and south to the Mississippi valley (circa 1600), copper was already being used. Thus, the stone age was gradually giving way to an era of metal: the processes of flaking and pecking, so characteristic of stone working, were being replaced by hammering and shaping of the copper nuggets – which had been torn from the copper-bearing rocks by glacial movement during the ice age. Whilst there is also evidence that copper was skillfully used in other regions (extending from Alaska to Florida), some of the most impressive items – celts, axes, spear-points and knives – are predominately from the Great Lakes and Mississippi River areas. A notable exception to this were the tribes of the Northwest Coast, who made superb copper items. Amongst the most distinctive of these were knives and daggers, many of which were highly decorated. However, the skills probably flowered with the introduction of refined copper obtained from white traders.[6]

The great value of metal over stone was clearly apparent and blades and knives were produced which were generally long, narrow, double-edged and had a convex cross-section, often not dissimilar to

those formerly of flint. The disadvantage of copper, however, was also clear to see – edges and points quickly blunted and, as cutting weapons, they had only limited value. It has been suggested that objects made of copper – and this included knives and daggers – were regarded as having particular and exceptional virtues, bordering on magical powers; indeed, certain early writers "aver that some of the tribes of the great lakes held all copper as sacred, making no practical use of it whatever."[7]

Knife symbolism

The symbolic nature of the knife was referred to by the traveler, Jonathan Carver, who made his way through Chippewa and Sioux country during the 1760s. Specifically referring to the Naudowessie (Santee Sioux), Carver reported that high-ranking warriors of that tribe carried a knife in a sheath decorated with porcupine quills and hung around the neck (p. 38). A point of interest is that the knife closely resembled the plug bayonet which was used by a number of [white] military forces in the seventeenth and early eighteenth centuries and, as Hanson observes, it was "also similar in some respects to the nineteenth-century "dag", or stabber knife."[8] (See p. 53.) Carver reports, however, that these distinctive knives were originally made of flint or bone but, with the availability of steel from the traders, they were now fabricated from metal. They were some 10 inches (25cm) in length, with the of the knife near to the handle almost 3 inches (7cm) wide; it was a double-sided keen-edge weapon which tapered to a sharp point.[9]

Although Carver refers to the custom as being a Sioux one, "a sword worn by the Chiefs of the Naudowessie," it possibly extended to at least the Chippewa, who also carried knives in a sheath suspended around the neck.[10] The Sioux, however, later put emphasis on retaining a triangular-type neck flap on fine buckskin "war" shirts which were worn by high-ranking individuals and such flaps resembled the original neck knife sheath.[11]

A century after Carver, the anthropologist Lewis Henry Morgan – who traveled up the Missouri in 1862 – made reference to the three oaths employed by the Plains tribes which they used to purge themselves from some charge. One of these oaths was swearing by the

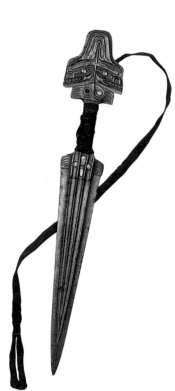

Left, above and right: *Examples of Northwest Coast knives which demonstrate the high skill in iron-working and decorative art developed by these groups in the nineteenth century. Left, a double-edged dagger. Above, a typical Tlingit war dagger, the handle decorated with a stylized animal emblem. Right, a two-bladed war knife collected from the village of Sitka. All three are Tlingit, dating from circa 1870.*

Left: *Eight styles of knives and knife sheaths from the Great Plains and Eastern Woodlands, dating from circa 1800–1900. Two of the upper sheaths are decorated with square shanked brass tacks. The blade of knife 2 is from a file, and has an elaborate horn handle. Both are identified as Blackfeet, circa 1875. The two central sheaths are beaded and the knives have wooden handles. Knife 3 is probably Cheyenne or Arapaho, circa 1870, 4 is possibly Santee Sioux, circa 1850. The superb presentation of knife 5 includes a horn handle and sheath embellished with quillwork. Probably Cree, circa 1830. Knife 6 is of Eastern Plains (Santee?) origin, circa 1840. Knife 7 could be a Menominee (?) quilled sheath, the horn handle exhibiting a finely carved turtle emblem, circa 1780. Knife 8 is a Blackfeet DAG with distinctive beaded sheath. The knife is circa 1810, the sheath circa 1880.*

knife. They raised "a knife in the right hand and point towards heaven saying 'I have stated the truth.' They then draw it between the lips and are required to touch the tongue to the blade. Those who swear falsely in this way attempt to avoid touching the tongue, which appears to be necessary to complete the oath."[12]

Knife symbolism, with complex ritualistic ceremonies, is perhaps nowhere better illustrated than with the Blackfeet Bear Knife Bundle. Although the style of knife used appears not to have been exclusive to the Blackfeet – their friends the Gros Ventre also had such knives – the rituals associated with the bear knife itself and its association with warfare appear highly developed by the Blackfeet.[13]

The chief object in the Bear Bundle was a large dagger-like knife, to the handle of which was attached the jaws of a bear. Although the power of such a knife was considered to be very great – so great "that its owner was seldom killed, for its appearance frightened everyone into submission, after the manner of bears"[14] – few individuals owned these bundles. One reason given was the brutality of the transfer ritual. Thus, the recipient was required to catch the knife thrown violently at him and also to lie naked on a thorn bed whilst being painted. At the same time, he was beaten with the flat of the knife.

In battle, the owner was not allowed to use any other weapon than the knife; he was required to walk forward towards the enemy, singing the war songs associated with the Knife Bundle and to never retreat. Little wonder that few warriors were prepared to shoulder such awesome responsibilities!

Knives of the Northwest Coast tribes

The distinctive copper knives referred to earlier as a feature of the Northwest Coast tribes were considerably elaborated upon with the introduction of iron and steel by the Russian, English and American traders who came in pursuit of profit in the lucrative maritime fur trade, which commenced in the late eighteenth century. The major demand was for the pelts of the sea-otter, an animal endowed with a lustrous coat of thick fur which "became by far the most valuable fur on the world market."[15]

In less than a decade, now potentially able to exploit the superiority of iron[16] over copper, the demand for the former metal was high

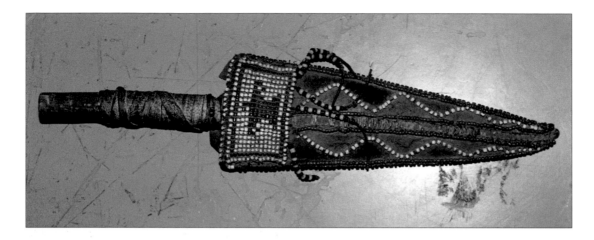

on the list of goods sought by the Northwest Coast tribes. In 1778, it is reported that the crewmen on Captain James Cook's third voyage traded "scraps of iron" for sea-otter skins[17]. Later came various trade goods of iron, such as pots, scissors, knives, axes and files, as well as pieces of iron and steel. This led to a new style of native industry where fish hooks, arrow and lance heads, chisel blades and daggers, were now fabricated from iron, rapidly replacing the use of bone, shell and stone.

The hand-fighting weapons, especially knives and daggers, were now developed to a high degree and those of the Northern tribes such as the Tlingit were particularly distinctive. A number were made from trade files, others from trade iron being hammered out on crude native forges. The blades were generally of a dagger form: some of the knives had a blade at each end, the smaller of which featured an animal head, the eyes being invariably inlaid with abalone shell. The handle was usually wrapped with heavy twine and then covered with tanned elk skin. Blades exhibited a midline ridge, concave or convex surfaces or were fluted, and the handles were nearly always terminated by the family or clan crest, such as a bear, beaver or Thunderbird.

These weapons were not only for show. Wearing moosehide shirts over which was an armor of rods or slats, and covering their bodies

Above: A fine knife and sheath, total length 14 inches (35cm), probably circa 1830 and from the Chippewa. The steel-bladed wooden handled knife is in a sheath decorated with pony beads and porcupine quills. The embellishments almost certainly make reference to sky and underwater powers.

from the neck to the knees, Tlingit warriors were formidable opponents. Especially with a war helmet and visor and with the fighting dagger in hand. The smaller blade was generally used to slash the face, so distracting the combatant; the larger blade was then employed to finish him off![18]

Another distinctive knife used by the Northern Northwest Coast tribes had a dagger-like blade and a spiral-hilt, sometimes described as "volute-handled" knives (p. 46). These, however, were almost certainly trade items, obtained from the Athapaskan tribes further to the north in the Yukon Valley. Tribes such as the Kutchin and Tanana made such knives either from old files or gun barrels; others were trade items from the Russians. The latter, however, were considered to have notable limitations in comparison to the native-made ones. The trader Alexander Hunter Murray observed of the Athapaskans who went to trade at Fort Yukon in 1848: "Their knives are made of iron, but the fancy handles and fluted blades are of more value to them than the temper of the knife; they complain of ours being too hard and the difficulty of sharpening them."[19]

Little is known about the native technology which produced these knives, which have been described as "most expert" and "sophisticated" – the metals in many specimens show both heat treatment and stress hardening.[20] The handles of the knives were wrapped with a split plaited cane or heavy elk skin and were carried either in the belt (p. 47) or in quilled or beaded knife sheaths, some of which might be hung around the neck,

Below: *An ornate sheath of heavy leather, decorated with blue, red and orange beadwork in the overlaid stitch. Note the triangular-shaped slot for attachment to the belt. This piece, which dates from circa 1880, was collected from the Sarcee.*

as described for the Chippewa and Sioux earlier. They were considered highly valued accoutrements in the Arctic and Subarctic regions.

Trade knives

The knives – which were traded by whites to the North American Indian in considerable numbers by the early 1600s – became both an indispensable tool and weapon.[21] The range of knives which were traded, even at this early period, was immense. The archaeological record documents both pocket and sheath knives, though the latter were generally of the type with a fixed and larger blade which was best for "heavy-duty cutting and for fighting."[22] Some of the best knives had fine bone handles, many inlaid with metal or horn. "Scalping" knives are listed in trade goods accounts; these generally had narrow blades which could be worked up between the skull and scalp after the initial incision had been made. In practice, however, almost any form of knife might be used.[23]

Two styles of knife which became particularly popular, and which appear to be predominately of English make, were the single-edged butcher or carving knife and the dagger. The former came in a wide variety of styles and many early ones were made in Sheffield and London, often bearing the maker's imprint. These included "Manson-Sheffield," "Lowcock of Cornhill (London)," "Wiggiams, Smithfield, London," and "V.R. (Victoria Regina) Sheffield".[24] One of the more distinctive of these trade knives seems to have been much coveted, probably because of its elaborately decorated handle of black horn and brass. Such a knife is shown (p. 48) in the series of knives offered by the Hudson's Bay Company and also in the portrait of the Menominee chief shown on p. 49.[25]

After about 1840, however, American knives began to displace the English variety. Many were produced by such companies as the John Russell Company at the Green River Works in Deerfield, Massachusetts, who started production as early as 1834.[26] These "Green River" knives became widely used trade items not only for hunting and warfare, but also for everyday use. Many were recycled; the steel blades, now often thin and sharply pointed, might be given new handles of horn or bone by the owner, a common type butcher knife then taking on a distinctive, personalized form.

Left: *A superb example of a volute-handled knife, dating from about 1860 and of a style used by the Subarctic Athapaskan groups such as the Kutchin and Tanaina of the Yukon-drainage region.*

Right: *A Kutchin warrior and his wife, after a sketch by Alexander Hunter Murray, who traveled to the Yukon in 1848. Note the volute-handled knife in the belt of the warrior, which is virtually identical to that shown on the left.*

Additionally, knives were fabricated by local blacksmiths, using a variety of iron-based metals. Each had its definite characteristics and the quality of the finished product was well recognized. Wrought iron, which was easily forged, produced good blades, but the edge and point dulled easily; cast iron held its edge and point better but was brittle, whilst steel in its various forms obviously maintained a good cutting edge – but was expensive. One old "knife saying" apparently, was "You can't always trust your neighbor, but you can always trust a good piece of steel."[27]

The "DAG" or "Beaver-Tail" knife

One distinctive style, initially introduced as a lance point, was the DAG. Known variously as the "beaver-tail knife," "Hudson's Bay DAG" or the "stabber," they were considered a favorite weapon for hand-to-hand combat.

DAG blades were first introduced in the Great Lakes area in the mid-1700s and soon became widely used. The long, wide blade was double-edged, coming to a sharp point, and resembled ancient styles of flint spear-heads. Indeed, one student has recently observed, "Perhaps the original designer fashioned these notched spears from the general shape of stone spear points found being used by the Indians."[28]

Above: *A series of trade knives which were offered by the Hudson's Bay Company during the fur trade era in Canada. Most of these knives were manufactured in Sheffield, with blades of high quality steel and handles of wood or bone. Some were elaborate and expensive, such as that on the extreme right. Here, the handle is brass, inlaid with horn.*

Right: *The Menominee chief, Kitchie-ogi-man, painted by Paul Kane in 1845. The use of the neck-knife is well illustrated here. Made of black-dyed buckskin and elaborately embellished with porcupine quills, it houses an English trade knife very similar to that shown above right.*

The blades were generally sold without handles, being manufactured in large numbers. Many were produced in England for the Hudson's Bay Company, becoming a standard and important item in the fur trade. Later, in 1821, when the Hudson's Bay Company merged with the North West Company (of Montreal), the simpler, thin-bladed DAG was replaced by a style which was thicker and exhibited a distinctive median ridge.[29] The handles, most of wood but some of bone or horn, were generally put on by their Indian owners, the double or single notches either side of the blade and near the tang facilitating the hafting. The exceptionally wide range of blades – which vary in both length, width, tang and notches – underlines the fact that many, as with the pipe tomahawk, were also manufactured

Below: An unusual sheath and knife, possibly Chippewa and dating from circa 1860. The knife appears to be made from an early style of French plug bayonet. The snakeskin, together with the beadwork designs, suggest a highly symbolic combination.

by local blacksmiths.[30]

Very fine versions of this knife, however, were also made as presentation pieces "much like presentation medals."[31] Examples of such knives are shown on pp. 42-53. Here, the handles are of black horn, with inlays of bone and brass. They were almost certainly made in Sheffield, England, and the main outlet in the early 1800s seems to have been through the Hudson's Bay Company.[32]

Peterson observed of these DAGS, that a "modern student of knife-fighting would reject these daggers as clumsy and inefficient."[33] Nevertheless, the Indian developed his own techniques: in combat, the knife was held with the blade below the hand and with a sidewise stroke he aimed at the ribs or stomach. Another method was a downward chopping-like stroke to stab behind the opponent's collar bone. In any event, a DAG-carrying warrior was, without doubt, a most formidable adversary!

Knife sheaths

While the blade of an Indian knife could well be of white manufacture, we have seen that the handles would often be adorned with the personal stamp of the owner – wood, bone, horn, antler and other material was subsequently used to haft the finished product.

Above: *A Bannock scout dressed in beaded shirt and leggings fringed with weasel and hair. Of particular interest here is the belt and knife sheath which are heavily studded with brass tacks and are very similar to those shown on p. 42.*

Similarly, the sheaths used to house the knives were, with few exceptions, of indigenous manufacture – the shape, materials used, as well as the mode of decoration were distinctively American Indian. The wide range of such sheaths is shown in both the Introduction and in this chapter.

The most common examples conformed to the shape of the most widely used blades – straight on one side, curved on the other. A distinctive feature of most Indian-made sheaths is a structural design

Left: *Five knife sheaths from as many regions. Top left: Subarctic Athapaskan, circa 1840. Top right: Eastern Plains, Hidatsa, circa 1860. Center, Great Lakes (note the quilled handle), circa 1760. Lower left: Northern Plains, Cree, circa 1870. Lower right: Crow(?), circa 1860.*

Above: *A Teton Sioux warrior wearing an elaborate quilled shirt from a painting by Zino Shindler, circa 1870. Knife symbolism is emphasized here; note the neck flap quillwork embellishment, which is almost certainly symbolic of knife handle and blade.*

which not only houses the blade but also the majority of the handle, only an inch or so being proud at the top of the sheath. This type of design obviously reduced the likelihood of losing the knife, particularly if – as in the case of many – a buckskin thong was tied around the protruding top of the handle.

Another relatively common sheath shape followed the contour of a DAG-type blade and was therefore curved on both sides. This shape is rather reminiscent of those sheaths which were hung around the neck (see Sioux knife symbolism, pp. 40-43 and also above).

Sheaths were decorated with porcupine quills and later, of course, with beads. On occasion, shells – particularly dentalium – were used

Left: *The Kansas warrior, Meach-o-shin-gaw, "Little White Bear," after a painting by George Catlin, 1832. Note that as with the previous portrait, the knife is prominently displayed – obviously symbolic of warrior prowess. The metal blade appears to be double-edged, the handle of wood with metal inlay.*

Below: *A superb presentation type DAG. These were manufactured in Sheffield, England, for the Hudson's Bay Company in the early nineteenth century. The handle is of black horn inlaid with bone and the sheath is decorated with loom quillwork. Almost certainly Cree, circa 1840.*

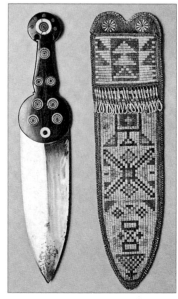

in combination with blue and red trade pony beads. Whilst such sheaths have been identified from the Missouri River region, they are of a style much favored by the Northern Athapascans, such as the Kutchin and Naskapi.[34]

An interesting feature of some knife sheaths is that a pattern of the blade and the handle is sometimes worked in quills or beads on the surface of the sheath. Although this feature does occur on the Cree(?) knife sheath shown on p. 52, it was particularly well developed by the Sioux and was commented on by the anthropologist, Frank G. Speck in papers relating to the structural basis to ornamentation amongst the Oglala.[35]

Above: *Early Blackfeet pictograph, circa 1830, of a warrior on horseback. Much detail is shown here, such as the scalp-lock and horse heart line. Of particular interest is the rendering of the warrior's gun, being captured; at the same time, he is stabbed in the chest with a large-bladed knife.*

Above right: *An early "bear knife." Although previously identified as Blackfeet, recent research (Klann,1999:45), suggests that it is actually of Assiniboin or Eastern Sioux origin. It was collected by Duke Paul Wilhelm of Württemberg, probably at Fort Union (1829–1831). The elaborate sheath is embellished with split bird-quills, an Eastern Plains rather than Northern Plains decorative art form.*

Sheaths for the early DAG were invariably ornamented with porcupine quillwork, wit both floral and geometric designs used. In the case of the latter, superb examples (such as that shown on p. 53) were embellished with bands of loom-woven quillwork, the finest of which – requiring very considerable skill – followed the pointed contour of the sheath.

Sword

There are many references in literature – descriptions, drawings, photographs and pictographs – of the use of swords by North American Indians. Many of them were probably English, Model 1796, light cavalry swords which were surplussed after the Napoleonic Wars. These were sold throughout the American West, and one outlet in the 1840s was the Bordeaux Trading Post near present-day Chadron, Nebraska.[36] They became a type of status symbol, particularly amongst some of the Plains tribes, perhaps in imitation of white soldiers – the Long Knives.

The establishment of authority by the use of the sword was described in the 1890s for the Yankton Sioux chief, *To-ka-cou*, "He that inflicts the first wound." Thus, on the arrival of distinguished visitors, chiefs such as *To-ka-cou* would take the strangers under their protection. Outside the visitors' lodge would be placed the chief's war club, or his sword; "the sign is well understood, and no Indian ventures to intrude."[37]

Sword, or sabre, symbolism extended to several other Plains tribes and possibly beyond. The Crow, for example, used sabres in the ceremonial-sacred context. The Crow leader, Wraps-Up-His-Tail, was said to have cut down pine trees with a sweep of his sword, "as he intended to do in mowing down the soldiers,"[38] and the focus of his supernatural power was said to be a red painted cavalry sabre. Swords, as well as lances, were proudly carried in mounted parades by the wives of successful warriors and were generally housed in beautifully decorated rawhide cases.[39]

Below: *A fine Bowie knife, the single-edged blade having the clipped point which is one distinctive feature of such knives. Although invented in America in the 1830s, many such knives were made in Sheffield, England. This one has a horn handle and was said to have belonged to the Hunkpapa Sioux leader, Sitting Bull.*

Above: *Crow sword or lance case, dating from circa 1890. Such cases – very typical of the Crow – were made of rawhide, cut into a form resembling that of a spade with a handle. The case was as shown here, decorated with incised designs, trade cloth and beads.*

Cases such as these were made of rawhide and were almost certainly invented by the Crow; it seems that they were exclusive to this tribe. Several factors also suggest that they were highly sacred in nature and for this reason they were not adopted by other tribes. Few were actually produced and they may well have had their origins in "an instructive dream or vision."[40]. Prior to the introduction of trade swords, these cases were exclusively used to house a lance. Hence the shape, which one student of the Crow has suggested is reminiscent of ancient styles of stone-pointed spears[41]. Generally, the cases exhibit a series of arrowhead-like symbols running sequentially along the case.[42] They are magnificent examples of Crow art.

Far left: *The Yankton Sioux chief, Moukauska, "Trembling Earth," from a portrait painted in Washington in 1837 by G. Cooke. Swords were carried and prominently displayed as a sign of status and authority. Although seldom employed in actual warfare, they could be used to symbolically protect strangers. Some were housed in decorative cases.*

CHAPTER THREE

Piercing Weapons

"The moon gave us the bow, the sun gave us the arrow"
(Pawnee legend)

*L*EAF-SHAPED CHIPPED STONE heads found in archaeological sites, as well as large points of bone and shell, give clear evidence that spears have long been used throughout North America, both as an implement of the chase or in warfare.[1] The spear appears to have developed into several varieties to match the environment, the habits of its animals and the warfare tactics employed. In the case of the

Right: *A petroglyph on rock, showing rider and horse, at Joliet, Montana. Probably produced by a Crow warrior in the early nineteenth century, it shows the rider carrying a bow-lance, combined piercing weapons of ancient origin.*

Eskimo, for example, who lived in a habitat characterized by a wide variety of animal life, a large number of spear forms were developed. In other areas, however, a simple form of spear was retained, although the point itself in historic times was made of trade metal and often of a more elaborate form.

Early descriptions of the use of spears by pedestrian tribes refer to a weapon as being some 5 or 6 feet (1.5m to 1.8m) in length. Blackfeet informants told the ethnologist John C. Ewers that such weapons – the head of which could be up to a foot (30cm) long – were attached to the end of a wooden shaft which was bound at intervals with otter fur to serve as grips. When used in hand-to-hand combat, the shaft was grasped with both hands, the warrior bringing it down with a quick, oblique downward stroke which combined both thrusting and swinging. As Ewers observed, "The weapon could kill or cripple an opponent if skillfully used."[2]

Above: Use of the atlatl (the Aztec word for "spear-thrower"). It is thought that Early Americans brought such devices across the Bering Strait at least 13,000 years ago. Used in both the hunt and war, they released the projectile with tremendous force to make the kill. The atlatl was one of the earliest compound weapons invented by man.

The atlatl

The need to effectively strike at a distance – to not only reduce personal danger but also to produce surer results – led to the development of a number of forms of propelling missile weapons by the American Indians. The sling, for example, was used extensively in Middle and South America and, to a more limited extent, by some of the Californian coastal tribes such as the Miwok and Pomo. Another weapon was the blow tube, which was used by the Cherokee, Choctaw, Seminole and other tribes in the Southeast where hollow cane could be easily obtained.[3]

More effective, however, was a weapon of ancient origin and with a very wide distribution. This was a special form of throwing stick which was generally referred to as a spear-thrower or atlatl. It is

Left: *The Assiniboin warrior,* Pitätapiú, *painted by the artist, Karl Bodmer, at Fort Union on the Upper Missouri in June 1833. He carries a ceremonial long bow-lance which is tipped with a metal head of a popular style and obtained from white traders. The lance is embellished with ribbons of soft, cured bear entrails which have been smeared with red sacred paint.*

almost certain that the spear-thrower was in use many thousands of years prior to the development of the bow. Indeed, it has been speculated that the ancestors of the American Indian brought the idea across the Bering Strait at least as early as thirteen thousand years ago. This would be some nine to ten thousand years prior to the introduction of the bow in North America.[4]

The atlatl was about 18 inches (45cm) in length and consisted of the main body – which was generally grooved on its upper side to take the spear shaft – the grip or handle and a hook or socket to engage with the end of the shaft. The basic design was greatly enhanced by carving, painting or other embellishments. Some of the most elaborate, such as those observed by Hernando Cortez amongst the Aztec, also seem to have "served as war clubs or shields as well."[5] The spear-thrower added an extra joint to the arm, thus increasing efficiency of the hurl; additionally, the forward momentum was markedly increased by attaching a stone weight to the main body of the atlatl.[6] Even after the invention of the bow, the atlatl had its advantages: not only could it project a missile which was several times heavier than an arrow but also, because only one hand was needed, it could be used more effectively from a canoe or kayak than the bow which, of course, demanded the use of both hands.

The atlatl was a lethal weapon in skilled hands. Thus, as one chronicler of the ill fated De Soto expedition observed of an Indian-Spanish encounter in the early 1540s: "One soldier was wounded with... a dart [which]... is thrown with a wooden strip or a cord. Our Spaniards had never seen this weapon before that day in any part of Florida through which they had traveled... The strip

Below: *The Crow warrior, He-who-jumps-over-everyone, painted by the artist George Catlin on the Upper Missouri in 1832. The long lance is typical for this period: the head could well be made from a cavalry sword blade, a popular item obtained from traders at an early period. Many were surplus after the Napoleonic Wars. Here, the lance was probably more for show than for practical use.*

Below: Keokuk, *chief of the Sauk and Fox Indians, with his son,* Musewont. *The elaborately decorated lance probably commemorates the killing of a distinguished mounted Sioux warrior. This portrait was painted during their trip to Washington in 1837.*

[atlatl] is of wood two-thirds of a yard in length, and is capable of sending a dart with such great force that it has been seen to pass completely through a man armed with a coat of mail. In Peru, the Spaniards feared this weapon more than any others the Indian possessed for the arrows there were not so fierce as those of Florida."[7]

The lance

Strictly speaking, this is a horseman's spear and was in general considerably longer than those used by pedestrian hunters and warriors. Although amongst some of the earliest groups to acquire the horse, the Plateau tribes appear not to have favored the use of a lance. For example, in the case of the Coeur d'Alêne – an important Salishan Plateau tribe – the spear, some 5 to 7 feet (1.5m to 2m) long and having a flint head, "went out of use as a weapon soon after the introduction of the horse and the beginning of buffalo hunting on the plains."[8] Likewise on the Northern Plains. Thus, the Piegan last made use of the lance in warfare in the 1860s.[9] By contrast, the Southern Plains tribes made very extensive use of this weapon in mounted warfare, possibly due to contacts with Spanish-Mexican soldiers, most of whom were highly skilled lancers. The Southern Plains tribes, however, as well as Southwestern tribes such as the Apaches, developed their own techniques of handling the lance in mounted combat. Of the Apache, for example, one observer commented, "they charge with both hands over their heads, managing their horses principally with their knees. With this weapon they are considered an overmatch for the Spanish dragoons single handed..."[10]

Comanche informants said that lance heads could be up to "thirty inches long by one inch wide (75cm by 2.5cm) tapering to a point at the end away from the shaft."[11] Lances, the Comanche said, were "never hurled javelin-wise but [were] always thrust from under the arm." Only a brave man carried such a weapon as it "meant hand-to-hand combat." The brother of the Comanche informant, Breaks Something, gave up his war lance after the Battle of Adobe Walls, much to the relief of his family, as all agreed such a weapon "is a big responsibility."[12]

With the passage of time the spear and lance, traditionally of important practical use, took on a religious significance – it began to be used in ceremonies and as society regalia, particularly amongst many Plains tribes. For this reason, the bow lance became the significant regalia of a number of distinguished individuals (see pp. 58 and 62).

The bow

Although, as we have seen, the atlatl was the most effective weapon in skilled hands, it was gradually replaced by a more portable and, in general, more accurate, projecting device – namely, the bow. Although irrefutable data is lacking, archaeological evidence suggests that the bow was "introduced into North America relatively recently – possibly as late as 1000 A.D.."[13] Nevertheless, by the time the first white man arrived in the Americas, it was a weapon which was widely distributed "from the far North to the tip of South America."[14]

The most commonly used bow type was the so-called self-bow, which was made of a single piece of hard, elastic wood. The type of wood depended on the locality but it was always "the best that could be found."[15] The self-bow seems to have been the only type employed

Above: *Little Smoke, a Sauk and Fox boy(?), carrying a bow and arrows. Boys were taught to use the bow at an early age, practising their skills by shooting small birds and animals. For safety, arrows were blunt-headed or had sticks bound crosswise on the lower part of the shaft.*

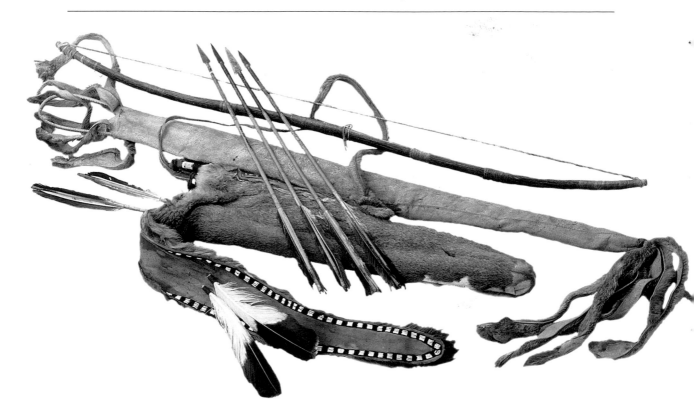

Above: *Combined bow-case and quiver with six arrows and bow. Collected from the Navajo in 1893. Mountain lion skin has been used to fabricate the combination which is hair-side out on the quiver. The tail of the mountain lion is pendant from the top of the arrow-case. The bow is of mesquite wood backed with sinew, the string of two-ply twisted sinew cord. It is 47 inches (1.2m) long.*

east of the Mississippi, it being an area of extensive forests which furnished abundant supplies of bow woods, such as ash, hickory and black locust. There was little need for alternative bow designs.

A similar bow type was the sinew-lined or reinforced bow. As with the self-bow, this consisted of a single stave of wood but as an addition the back was covered with a thin sheet of sinew which was securely glued to the surface. Such bows, unlike the eastern self-bow which could be up to 6 feet (1.8m) in length, seldom exceeded 45 inches (1.2m); they were widely used on the Great Plains as well as in California.

These styles contrast markedly in the Arctic region. Here, the Inuit people needed to make do with what was to hand. Drift, and other wood pieces, were ingeniously joined together, the joints being reinforced with splints, bridges and wedges, and the weapon then bound and backed with a complexity of braided and twisted sinew cords – hence the description "sinew corded bow." It was a style used "almost exclusively by the Eskimo."[16]

Similar in some respects because of the complexities of production, was the so-called "compound bow" which was made of antler, horn, baleen or bone, backed with a heavy lining of sinew. These bows were much favored by the Plateau tribes, although they were not entirely exclusive to that region.

The self-bow

Some of the carliest illustrations (c.1585) by John White of the Indians of present-day North Carolina and Virginia, show bows which, at a conservative estimate, were 5 feet 6 inches to 6 feet (1.7m to 1.8m) in length. Of relatively simple construction and resembling the English longbow, they were undoubtedly of a style which extended back at least a further 500 years. Within a century of contact with whites, however, the bow was being rapidly replaced by the gun. As one scholar has observed, "it can safely be said that by 1700 every Indian from the Atlantic to the Mississippi had heard of

Below: Bow, quiver and arrows, collected from the Makah of Neah Bay in the Olympic Peninsula, circa 1870. The bow, some 46 inches (1.2m) in length, is made of yew with the grip of a wrapping of bark. It is the same form as the bows used further south and inland but it lacks the sinew backing. The cedar bone-headed arrows are contained in a wooden (cedar?) quiver. Note the carved head of a wolf – probably evoking shamanistic powers.

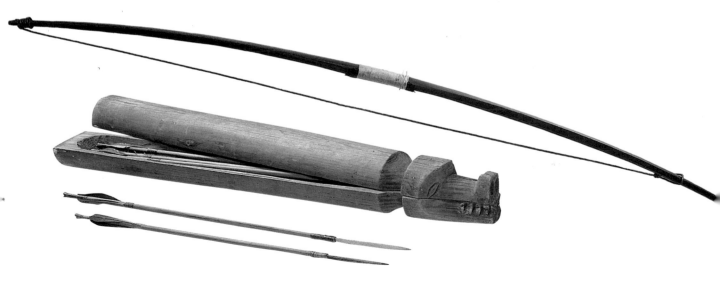

MAKING AN ARROW

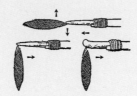

(i) Knocking off chips from obsidian by free hand or direct percussion – the first step in shaping.

(ii) Pressing off flakes from a portion of obsidian by means of a bone flaker.

(iii) Shaping the flint arrowhead with a bone tool; on occasions, bone pincers were used.

(iv) An alternative method of flaking, the operator holding the head upon a stone.

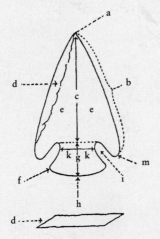

Left: *Arrowhead nomenclature. (a) Point (b) Edge (c) Face (d) Bevel (e) Blade (f) Tang (g) Stem (h) Base (i) Notch (k) Neck (m) Barb or Shoulder. The majority of arrowheads were notched; these were set in a slot at the end of the arrowshaft and tied in place with sinew or cord which was passed through the notches and around the end of the arrowshaft.* **Right:** *A finished flint arrowhead showing the attachment cord running through the notch.*

Above: *A high quality finished arrow, probably Mandan, a tribe who were particularly well known for their skill as arrow-makers.* **Left:** *An arrow-straightener of bone, from the Mandan village of Ruhptare on the Missouri River 1837.*

the gun and was clamoring for one, and the art of making good bows went into a rapid decline."[17]

Astonishingly, except for one archaeological find of a badly decomposed bow, only one other bow of early and good provenance, from this area is to be found in the collections. Referred to as the "Sudbury bow"[18] and identified as Wampanoag – a tribe who greeted the Pilgrim Fathers at Plymouth, New England, in 1620 – it is nearly 5 feet 6 inches (1.7m) in length, made of hickory and finely finished. A replica of this bow, made in the 1920s, was found to have a "weight of 46 pounds at 28 inches of draw and a cast of 173 yards." It was described as "soft and pleasant to shoot, and could do effective work either as a hunting or a war implement."[19] Clearly, much was lost with the introduction of the gun, not least stealth in hunting or approaching the enemy, but it is obvious that as far as the eastern tribes were concerned, the advantages of ball and powder outweighed the arrow and bow in a woodland environment – far less so in other regions.

The sinew-lined bow

Often referred to as a sinew-backed bow, this type of bow was popular on the Great Plains and, unlike the Eastern Woodlands, it was retained when firearms were introduced to the Plains region, being particularly effective on horseback. Such bows, seldom more than 3 feet 6 inches (1.1m) in length, had layers of finely shredded sinew glued on the back, as Mason describes it, "laid on so that it resembles bark."[20] A Blackfeet bow described in the 1920s is typical of the

Below: *The techniques of arrow release, where the arrow nock is held a certain way and then let loose in the shooting. As shown here, four techniques were used by Indian tribes north of Mexico: the tertiary release was most commonly employed by the Plains tribes. The three others were used in the Northeast and Southwest.*

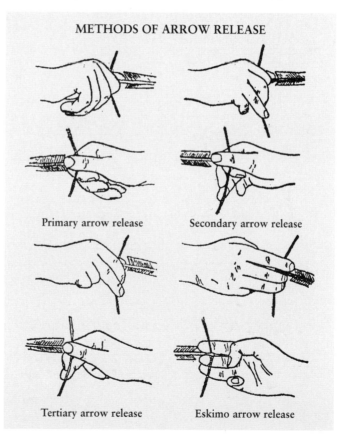

METHODS OF ARROW RELEASE

Primary arrow release

Secondary arrow release

Tertiary arrow release

Eskimo arrow release

Left: *Two Yuma men photographed circa 1870. The man on the left holds a skillfully shaped strung bow in his left hand, together with several arrows. The arrows appear to be of a hard wood-tipped type, probably for hunting small game and birds. This tribe, together with others in the Southwest, such as the Mohave and Pima, mainly used a specialized form of club in warfare; bows were thus not well developed. Such bows were generally made of cottonwood and unbacked. They were ineffective in warfare and renowned more for their beauty than practical use.*

Above top: *A Ceremonial bow and single arrow, collected from the Haida at Skidegote, in 1883. The elaborate carvings on these unique pieces probably make reference to family history and would be carried during tribal ceremonials.*

Above bottom: *A ceremonial bow from the Chippewa or Ottawa of the Michigan region and dating from the mid-nineteenth century. It is embellished with carvings of three otters, one of which is emerging from the water with a fish, symbolic of good hunters and protective spirits.*

Plains style for the mid-nineteenth century. Up to 3 feet 4 inches (1m) in length, it was of a flat oval cross-section. The sinew lining tended to draw it into a reflexed position when not braced. The string was of two strands of twisted sinew, tied with half-hitches in the lower nock and a slipknot at the upper nock. Even though of considerable age, when it was braced it was found to be "a springy, vigorous weapon" and when "drawn 20 inches it weighs 40 pounds and shoots 153 yards."[21]

A wide variety of woods were used on the Plains to make the sinew-lined bow; unlike the self-bow where the elasticity of the wood determined the bow's characteristics, it was the sinew which was the main contributing factor to the weight of the lined bow rather than the wood itself. As long as the wood was able to withstand the compression which occurred on drawing the arrow, requirements were largely satisfied. Suitable woods were continually sought. As Mason observed more than a century ago, "it has been often averred that an Indian was always on the lookout for a good piece of wood… These treasures were put into careful training at once, bent, straightened, steamed, scraped, shaped, whenever a leisure moment arrived. No thrifty Indian was ever caught without a stock of artillery stores."[22]

The Hidatsa, Wolf Chief, himself a skilled bowyer, said that chokecherry, wild plum, cedar and iron-wood was not infrequently used; however, ash was one of the most popular woods since it was relatively abundant on the Plains. A limb or trunk some 3 inches (7cm) in diameter was generally cut in the winter but the right raw material was not easy to find and indeed one modern scholar of the Plains bow expressed the opinion that the "rarity of usable wood of sufficient length and straightness might be one of the reasons for Northern Plains bows being mostly short."[23]

The bows made by many of the tribes in California and were structurally similar to the Plains sinew-lined bow. However, at mid-limb, the width was generally greater than that of a Plains bow and yew or juniper – rather than ash – was commonly used. A distinctive feature of the coastal California bows was that many were elaborately painted with repeating geometrical designs such as diamonds, triangles and bands, generally in blue and red. As has been observed, "These California bows, as a class, excite the admiration of anyone who has every made a successful self-bow."[24]

The horn bow
As discussed earlier, the power of a sinew-lined bow pivoted largely on the sinew which was attached to the back of the bow. When drawn, the sinew was stretched and the wood of the bow limbs which supported it was compressed. The thicker the sinew layer, the more powerful the bow. However, there is a limit to the amount of compression wood can withstand; beyond that, it permanently deforms and can no longer support the sinew-lining for efficient action.[25]

The problem was largely overcome by the use of horn, which can withstand far higher compression than wood. Thus, layers of the sinew lining were built up to far greater thicknesses, giving a proportional increase in bow strength. Such bows were often surprisingly short, certainly very seldom greater than 3 feet 4 inches (1m), with the majority in the region of 3 feet (90cm).[26] They were impressively powerful for their size. As the traveler Alfred Jacob Miller commented in 1834 when he observed Shoshone warriors using such bows, "With an Elk-horn bow, they sometimes drive an

Above: A Karok warrior of northern California, wearing rod armor. He is carrying a short wooden bow and several metal-tipped arrows in a quiver under his right arm. Note the technique employed for holding a reserve arrow for quick release!

Right: A combined Hupa (1885) bow and arrow-case. It is made of a complete coyote skin. The arrows are typically northern Californian.

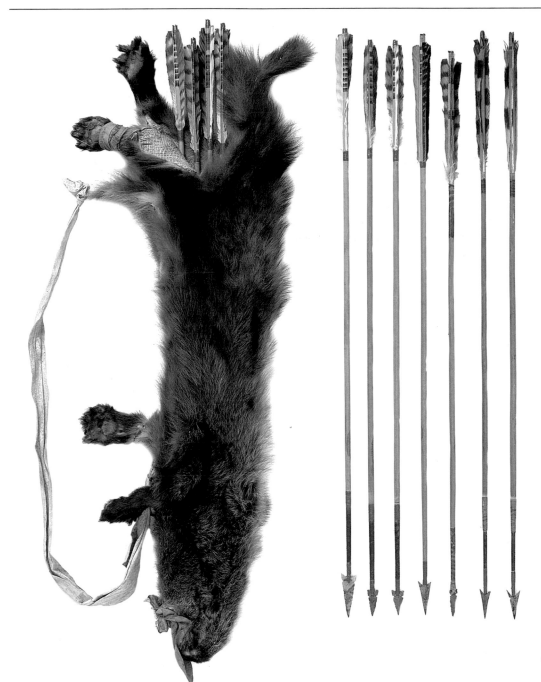

arrow completely through a Buffalo, its propelling power being greater than that of a Yew bow'.[27]

The making of the horn bow, one scholar has commented, is "among the great triumphs of human ingenuity... Because of the limitations under which the Indian bowyer had to work, it is only natural to wonder how he managed to produce such a weapon."[28] The tools available to prepare the horn were limited and, prior to the introduction of metal knives and hatchets, it is highly probable that very few, if any, horn bows were produced. A date of 1700 has been suggested for the first appearance of the horn bow and this coincides well with the arrival of trade knives and other tools in great numbers to the Plateau tribes.[29]

The horn used was from the elk or mountain sheep ram; with their complex turns and twists, neither satisfy the criteria suggested by Faris and Elmer who, in their detailed studies of horn bows, commented that "a prime requisite of the horn for a bow should be that in its original state on the head it should have only a simple curvature in one plane."[30]

The techniques of construction of an elk horn bow were described by the Hidatsa, Wolf Chief, who, as a fifteen-year-old teenager, had watched his father, Small-ankles, make one over a period of some two weeks. The horns, which were picked up after being shed, first had the tines cut off; then the horn was worked down with a sharp knife to an even thickness. It was now heated in a soil trench for some twenty-four hours, which softened the horn and allowed it to

Below: *Apache warriors photographed circa 1880. All armed, the righthand warrior carries a flintlock gun, the others more traditional weapons – lance and bow. Note the long arrow, so typical of the Apache, held by the central figure. The shafts were generally of reed, the foreshaft of a harder wood.*

be further worked down, shaped and then polished. Two bow limbs were so produced and these in turn were spliced together. The notches for the bow string were cut. Then, after scoring the back of the horn, layers of shredded sinew were successively built up with glue between each layer, so producing a sinew back which, on most bows, was "approximately half the total thickness of the limb."[31] The twisted sinew bow string was attached permanently at one end whilst a loop at the other end of the string enabled the bow to be braced for use.[32]

The procedure for making a mountain sheep horn bow was similar, the main criteria being a crush resistant platform to which the elastic sinew could be attached.[33]

As already mentioned, Alfred Jacob Miller (1834) was clearly greatly impressed with the horn bow, not only in the very efficient use

Above: *Armed Californian Indians, probably Hupa, circa 1840. In addition to the interesting rendering of hair-styles, the arrow, the technique of release and the details of the bow (with the broad middle tapering towards the ends), are accurate for the Hupa. The quiver is very similar to that shown on p. 71.*

of it by his Shoshone companions but also by the obvious skill which went into its making.[34] He observed: "Now if an Elk-horn was carried to the smartest Yankee we have, with a request to make a bow of it, the probability is, that, for once, he would not find it convenient to attempt it."[35]

Arrows

The structure of an arrow is made up of six parts: nock, feathering, shaftment, foreshaft, shaft and head. Each differed in technique of assemblage, materials used, sizes and decoration, according to the region in which it was made. Arrow-making was a skilled occupation involving such activities as the selection of the wood, straightening and polishing the shaft, cutting and attaching the feathers and arrowhead, shaping the nock and notch, and channeling or painting the shaft and shaftment.[36] All required lengthy experience and practise to ensure the production of an effective missile which would have a devastating effect on animal or man.

During the period of the Plains Indian wars, considerable interest was taken by army surgeons and others regarding the power of the bow and the wounds inflicted by arrows. Many stories were related in regard to the force of arrows shot by Indian bowmen and several border on the bizarre. An example is the case of the Kiowa chief, Satamore, who, in 1862 near Fort Larned, Kansas, was wounded after being shot in the buttocks by a Pawnee. The shaft was withdrawn but it left the arrowhead in his body. Satamore passed bloody urine but the wound healed quickly and within a few weeks he was able to go on the hunt for buffalo. For more than six years he continued at the head of his band, "leading it in all its travels and adventures or the chase."[37] The presence of the arrowhead, however, troubled him somewhat and in August 1869 he conferred with a military surgeon at Fort Sill. On examination it was revealed that the arrowhead had

Above: *Three iron-headed Comanche arrows, collected in the 1860s. The 26 inch (63cm) shafts are of osier engraved with nearly straight "lightning" channels. The shaftments taper to the back and are banded with red and green paint; the nocks are swallow-tail shape.*

Left: *A fine Sioux or Cheyenne bow, collected by the Italian traveler, Antonio Spagni, circa 1850. Some 40 inches (1m) in length, it is embellished with trade beads and has a string of twisted sinew. This bow and twenty arrows, was collected with the quiver shown on p. 78.*

Below: *An Arapaho plain bow, dating circa 1870, of ovoid cross-section, tapering towards the ends, and some 48 inches (1.2m) long.*

penetrated deep into Satamore's bladder producing a large vesical calculus. Two surgeons performed a lithotomy and the calculus was removed. It was more than 2½ inches (6.2cm) in length and, when cut in two, revealed the presence of the arrowhead as its nucleus. All evidence suggests that Satamore fully recovered from this somewhat unpleasant sequence of events – set in train by the Pawnee arrow some seven years before!

Others were less fortunate, such as Private Spillman of the 7th Cavalry who was wounded by a Kiowa war-party in a skirmish which took place near Fort Dodge, Kansas, in June 1867. The soldier received three arrow wounds, the worst going through the right lumbar region and penetrating some 8 inches (20cm) into the abdominal cavity. With difficulty, the arrow was removed; however, the wound proved mortal.[38]

In less severe cases, Indians had their own techniques of removing arrowpoints when embedded in the body. A willow stick was split, "the pith scraped out, and the ends rounded so that they may readily follow the arrow track. The pieces are introduced so as to reach and cover the barbs; they are then adjusted, bound to the arrowshaft, and all withdrawn together."[39]

Tribal origin, and perhaps even a particular craftsman in some notable cases, could often be identified.[40] Thus, in 1833, when writing of Plains Indian types of weaponry, the German traveler Maximilian, observed: "Though all their arrows appear, at first sight, to be

POWER OF THE ARROW

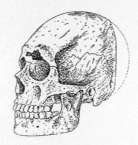
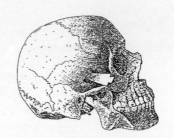

Skull of US cavalryman pierced by Comanche iron arrowhead, near Fort Concho, Texas.

Skull of a Mexican killed in an Indian fight 75 miles notrhwest of Fort Concho, Texas, 1868.

Skull of a white man pierced by arrowpoint in Indian fight near Pecos River, Texas, 1870.

Below: *The effect of a steel-headed arrow on the human body. A pierced vetebra found on Little Bighorn, 1877.*

perfectly alike, there is a great difference in the manner in which they are made. Of all the tribes of the Missouri the Mandans are said to make the neatest and most solid arrows. The iron heads are thick and solid, the feathers glued on, and the part just below the head, and the lower end, are wound round with very even, extremely thin sinews of animals... The Manitaries make the iron heads thinner, and not so well... The Assiniboins frequently have very thin and indifferent heads to their arrows, made of iron-plate."[41]

Arrowshafts were of straight wood, stems, cane or reeds depending on the region.[42] A notable exception was in the Arctic where the shaft might be of pieces of bone or driftwood bound together with sinew. Owing to the scarcity of materials, the shafts of arrows in this region were generally short, although the foreshaft which served the double purpose of making the front of the arrow heavier than the rear and gave a more effective means of attaching the arrowhead, tended to extend the overall length of a typical Arctic arrow.

The shaftment of the arrow – that part of the shaft upon which the feather is fastened – varied greatly in length, form and ornamentation. It was this part of the weapon upon which bands, and other marks, often for identification purposes, were usually placed.

As is well known, feathering is an important feature of any arrow, its main function being to retard the rear end of the missile and cause it to move straight. Thus, most North American arrows were fletched, generally with two or three split feathers.[43] An alternative, however, was to use a relatively massive head on the arrow which also served to keep the missile straight. Such was the case with some Eskimo groups who, with an elaborate foreshaft/arrowhead combination, dispensed with fletching altogether. This contrasts markedly with arrows from the Plains and Southwest region where the fletching feathers on the shaftment were often 6 inches (15cm) or more in length.

Most arrowpoints were usually made of some material firmer and heavier than the shaft. Not only, of course, did it give greater penetrating power to the arrow, but it also tended to increase both the accuracy and range. Many arrowheads were of flint and other varieties of stone, as well as horn, bone, antler, wood, shell and copper. The last was used by tribes in the region of Lake Superior and to a lesser extent by those in Alaska and British Columbia. Shapes were usually triangular and mostly notched to facilitate attachment in a slot at the end of the shaft, the head generally being tied with sinew which passed through the notches.

Stone arrowheads were produced with great skill and patience by a process of chipping and flaking (p. 66); of a naturally brittle material, they were liable to shatter on impact and for this reason those made of iron rapidly replaced the earlier, natural materials.[44]

Quivers and bow-cases

The style of quiver and bow-case varied greatly from one region to the next. Not only did it depend on the size of the bow and arrows but also on materials readily available. Sealskin was used in the Arctic by such groups as the Central Eskimo; on the West Coast, some quivers

Above: *Cheyenne warrior, circa 1880. A combined bow-case and quiver is being carried with the strap across the left shoulder. The combination is of buffalo hide with the hair-side out. Similar examples are extant in the collections.*

Above: *A superb combined bow-case and quiver, partially made of otter hide and embellished with blue and white pony beads. This was collected by the Italian traveler, Antonio Spagni, in about 1850, who identified it as Sioux. Such arrow and bow-cases, with the long decorated triangular flap, were popular items at this time.*

Above right: *A fine Plains Indian combined bow-case and quiver, with arrows (Assiniboin?). Made of buffalo hide, it dates from the second half of the nineteenth century (circa 1860–70). It is decorated with blue and pink seed beads and red trade cloth which has possibly been cut from a British officer's uniform.*

Right: *A fine combined bow-case and quiver made of otter skin with the fur-side out. Dating from circa 1880, it was originally identified as Nez Perce, but is probably Crow. The buckskin is embellished with red, blue, green and white beads. Length of bow-case is 20 inches (50cm).*

Below: *A bow-case and quiver with associated arrows and bow (Sioux?). Made of buffalo hide with the fur-side out, it was collected by the traveler Friedrich Köhler, about 1830. Both bow-case and quiver are bound with red trade cloth and decorated with blue pony beads.*

were of cedar wood whilst various animal skins and pelts were used by the Plateau, Plains and Woodland tribes and also to a lesser extent by those groups in the Southwest, who sometimes also used soft basketry.

Styles varied considerably, but the most common was a combined bow-case and separate arrow-case which were laced together and which generally had a strap which went over the shoulder. Some bow-case-quiver combinations were particularly elaborate, such as the elegant and richly decorated ones made from three otterskins with two heavily beaded flaps attached – one at the mouth of the bow-case, the other on the arrow-case. Such magnificent accoutrements have been firmly associated with both the Plateau and Plains tribes, particularly the Nez Perce and Crow.[45] (See Plate, p. 79).

CHAPTER FOUR

Defensive Weapons

Auotani
(Blackfeet for "shield")

FOLLOWING CHRISTOPHER COLUMBUS' first voyage to the "new" American continent in 1492, the Spanish, under Juan Ponce de León, skirted the coast of a region known as *Bimini*. It was Easter Week – *Pasque Florida* – and that name became attached to an area of the Southeast which is now known as Florida (but at the time also included parts of present-day South Georgia and East Carolina). The date was May 1513. On the west coast, in the vicinity of present-day Tampa Bay, the Spanish sailed into a natural harbor. Here, they met the Calusa, a powerful tribe which dominated the region.[1]

The use of body armor

What repeatedly comes through in reports from the Spanish and later from the French and English, is that the Calusa were fierce and determined fighters, that warfare was very much a way of life and that their offensive weapons – bows, clubs, perhaps also the spear and atlatl – and their warfare tactics, were very effective against most enemies. There is, however, little data regarding the Calusa's defensive weapons.[2]

In addition to the sword, lance, and later the gun, the Spaniards were well aware of the value of body armor, the conquistadors commonly wearing metal breast and back plates as well as a "kettle" hat, chin plates and sometimes leg-guards. It is probable that the use of this type of protective weaponry, as was the case later in the

Right: *Tlingit armour collected in 1880 (but probably considerably older than this date), combining two styles – wood slats and rods. Such armor was restrictive to body movement but the heavy slats offered considerable physical protection. Use of rods under the arm sections, however, gave a higher degree of flexibility and rawhide strips, together with sinew cords, bound slats and rods together.*

Far left: *A Huron warrior from an early eighteenth century print. He wears armor made from slats of wood bound together with cords. Both chest and back are adequately covered. Effective against enemy arrows, such armor rapidly fell into disuse with the introduction of firearms.*

Spanish Southwest, on the Northwest Coast and in Alaska, was adopted and modified by the Calusa and other tribes in the region, utilizing the native materials readily available to them.

This possibility aside, however, there is also good evidence to suggest that various forms of body protection were independently developed by North American Indians. If the early renderings which we have of such armor are to be believed much, and perhaps not surprisingly, it was similar in basic design – chest and back covering, helmets, leg and even chin plates (p. 81) – to that worn by the Europeans.[3]

Left: *Shield bearing warriors depicted in pictographs on rock in Montana. Probably of Shoshone or Kutenai origin, and dating from at least 1750, these show the large shields and weaponry carried in pedestrian warfare.*

Below: *In addition to the slat armor worn by Huron warriors (p. 80), they carried large circular shields made of cedar bark, as shown in this early engraving. Note the substantial carrying straps and that the shield covers both head and body.*

An illustration attributed to F. J. Bressani, and produced prior to 1660, shows a Huron warrior wearing armor made of tightly laced osier rods or bark strips, the unit tightly laced together with sinew or buckskin thongs.[4] More than half a century later, it had not radically changed (p. 80).

Styles of body armor

Native American armor has been categorized into five basic types, which were largely determined by materials available in a particular region. For example, that of the Inuit and Eskimo groups, where wood was particularly scarce, was generally made of overlapping plates of bone, ivory and later – after contact with whites – of iron.[5] On the Northwest Coast, California and, as has been discussed, to the east amongst the Huron as well as the Iroquois and Indians of Virginia, body armor was either wooden slats or rods tightly bound together.

Body garments of hardened or multilayered hides were widely used, being attributed to Northwest Coast tribes such as the Haida, Chinook and Tlingit as well as to Plateau and Plains tribes (Shoshone and Pawnee). This armor style has also been described for such widely

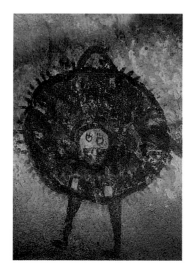

spaced tribes as the Mohawk to the east of Lake Ontario and the Navajo more than three thousand air miles to the Southwest in present-day New Mexico.[6]

The impact of the gun

The various, largely indigenous, armor styles were effective against native weaponry but far less so against gun-armed opponents and although the impacting ball would lose some of its power, native armor rapidly fell into disfavour with the advent of the gun. As the Blackfeet, Weasel Tail, observed to the ethnologist John Ewers, armor was adequate protection against arrows but it was unable to ward off bullets from early firearms. Consequently, the Blackfeet "abandoned its use after their enemies became armed with guns."[7] This was a sentiment implied, if not stated, in other regions and, largely for this reason, such armor fell into disfavour, becoming a relic of the past. However, in the case of one dominant Plains tribe, the Sioux, it was

Above: *A pictograph – paint on a rock surface – depicting a pedestrian shield-bearing warrior in present-day Wheatland County, Montana. Note the similarity to the Huron warrior (p. 82). Many of the shields in this type of rock art display, as here, the medicine signs of the shield owner.*

Right: *One of three large rawhide shields found in a cave near Torrey in Utah in 1925. Carbon 14 techniques date them from circa A.D. 1500. Almost 3 feet (1m) in diameter, these enhance details in the style shown in early pictographs (pp. 82 and 83). Note the elaborate symbolic paintings.*

Above: *A Cheyenne warrior dressed in the regalia of the Red-Shield Society, one of the five original warrior societies of the great Prophet. He carries the distinctive shield of the Society made from a buffalo hide with the tail left on. The shirt is reminiscent of the early style, pedestrian body armor.*

retained as a single-layered, decorated garment and became the symbol of high-ranking office, that of "Shirt Wearer."[8] (See "Symbolic weapons.")

Early styles of shield
Rectangular-shaped shields
Early descriptions of the shields used in North America refer to a large circular style made of heavy hide, basketry, wooden rods or bark, or heavy multilayered elk hide. There were, however, some notable exceptions. Thus, a shield collected in the 1930s from Kagamil Island – one of the Aleutian Islands – and made sometime prior to white contact, is actually rectangular. Made of two heavy wooden boards laced together with thongs, it is embellished with geometrical designs – obviously highly symbolic to the owner – rendered in red paint.[9]

South of the Plateau region, amongst such tribes as the Coeur d'Alêne and Okanagon, several ancient styles of shields have been described, one of which was oblong and about 5 feet (1.5m) long. It was made of a single piece of heavy elk hide and was said to "sometimes [be] moistened with water when about to be used" and that "one side often carried painted designs."[10] None of the oldest living Indians amongst these tribes, however, could remember the use of these ancient forms of shields, observing that they "went out of use after horses were employed, as they were not adapted for riding."[11]

The circular shield
In addition to the slat armor described earlier, the Huron also carried circular shields.[12] These shields were at least 3¹/₂ feet (1.2m) in diameter with two carrying handles and, it appears, had a wooden hoop around the circumference (p. 82). Some two centuries later, in the 1720s, Lafitau described the Iroquoian styles of shield: "Their

shields were of ozier or bark covered with one or many *peaux passées*; there are some made of very thick skin. They had them of all sizes and all sorts of figures."[13]

Shields of this type were well suited to pedestrian warfare, as illustrated by the many petroglyphs and pictographs found on rock faces throughout the Plateau and Plains region. Most conspicuous are the large shields carried by the pedestrian warriors together with long bows, spears and clubs. The shields were up to 3 feet (1m) in diameter and are shown embellished with designs which probably represented the protectors and helpers of the warriors who carried them. Some of these designs are semirealistic, others more abstract, suggestive of the development of a complex system of symbolism.

Below: *Horse armor, probably Crow, circa 1870. Such accoutrements seem to have been of indigenous origin and unrelated to Spanish type horse armor which was used on the Southern Plains. The discs exhibit symbolic paintings suggesting the evoking of the sky's protective powers aided the actual mechanical protection of the rawhide itself.*

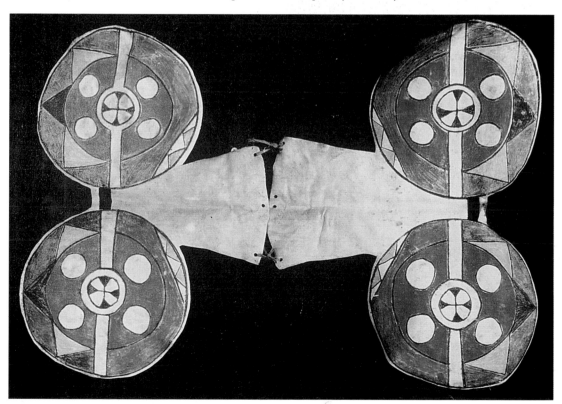

85

Left: Keokuk *or "The Watchful Fox," chief of the Sauk and Fox. Portrait from life by George Catlin when he visited Keokuk's village in 1834. Less nomadic equestrian people than the Plains tribes further west, Catlin's portrait suggests that the Sauk and Fox retained the large, early type of rawhide shield so typical of early pedestrian warriors (pp. 82 and 83). Here, Keokuk carries a shield (some 3 feet (1m) in diameter) on his left arm, together with a highly decorated staff of office.*

These shield-bearing warrior motifs are particularly numerous at rock art sites on the Northwestern Plains and generally predate the appearance of the Blackfeet alliance.[14] These warrior figures were almost certainly of Shoshone and Kutenai – tribes who dominated the Northern Plains area prior to circa 1740.[15] Support for this suggestion comes from the finding in 1925 of three large hide-painted shields, in a dry cave near Torrey, Utah. Referred to as the "Pectol shields" – after the finder Ephraim Pectol – mass spectrometry and radio carbon techniques date them to circa A.D. 1500.[16] Arm loops at the back of each shield, similar to those shown on the Huron shield (p. 82), offered some support, but the greater weight, it appears, was eased with a neck strap.[17]

Such shields were certainly not exclusive to the prehistoric Northwestern Plains. Early Spanish explorers on the Southern Plains describe "large buffalo hide shields to cover the entire body,"[18] whilst early painted hides rediscovered in Switzerland some fifty years ago, show pedestrian warriors (probably Plains Apache), their torsos entirely hidden behind their shields.[19]

The designs on the Pectol shields, as well as those documented in Rock Art, suggest ancient traditions of extensive religious concepts and mythology of the type identified by Clark Wissler and Robert H. Lowie for the historic Plains tribes[20]... protective and other designs associated with sky and earth powers, animal powers, metamorphosis and even, perhaps, lunar designs.[21]

As was discussed earlier ("The use of body armor"), a form of hide body armor was worn by the pedestrian Plains tribes: this, together with the large rawhide shields, made them formidable opponents. A battle between similarly armed groups which took place about 1720, was described by the elderly Saukamappee, an adopted member of the Piegan who were moving into the Plains and progressively forcing the Shoshone to retreat to the Rocky Mountains. It refers to the method of using large shields and their effectiveness against arrows.

Warfare by pedestrian shield-bearing warriors

A combined force of some three hundred and fifty Cree and Piegan were confronted by a similar number of Shoshone in the vicinity of the Eagle Hills in present-day Southwest Saskatchewan. A few guns were owned by the Piegan but, because of the shortage of ammunition, these were reserved for hunting. Thus, both sides were armed with ancient styles of offensive and defensive weapons – lance, bows and arrows and large shields. There was much pre-battle ceremonial feasts in a great War Tent, together with speeches and dances. A war chief was selected who then led the foot warriors towards the Shoshone. Saukamappee related: "Both parties make a great show of their numbers, and I thought that they were more numerous than ourselves. After some singing and dancing, they sat down on the ground, and placed their large shields before them, which covered them: We did the same, but our shields were not so many, and some of our shields **had to shelter two men**" (author's stress.)[22] Saukamappee described the Shoshone bows as superior to their own; generally, they were shorter and sinew-backed. Their arrows, however, were less effective as they had flint heads which shattered on impact, whilst those of the Piegan and Cree were of iron, the arrows sticking into the rawhide shields but not penetrating them. Several were wounded on both sides. but none severely, and nightfall put an end to the battle. Saukamappee reported that not a scalp was taken on either side and observed, somewhat wryly, "in those days such was the result."[23]

This was not always the case, however, for at other times, after a period of relatively ineffective archery fire, another stage might be the substitution of "shock for fire."[24] The war chief led the whole line in a charge; often, this was preceded by the singing of a war song, the

Above: *A warrior on horseback, both horse and man covered with hide armor. Writing-On-Stone in the Milk River Valley of southern Alberta. Possibly Shoshone, sometime prior to 1800. The Shoshone are the only Northwestern Plains/Plateau tribe to have used this style of horse armor, which is probably an influence from their relatives, the Comanche in the south.*

Left: *A Tonkawa Indian, circa 1830. The Tonkawa were neighbors of the powerful Comanche, and this gun-carrying warrior is dressed in an attenuated form of body armor which gave freer movement on horseback than earlier styles. These garments were described as being painted red, green or blue; further decoration on this example seems to be porcupine quillworked discs.*

charge itself being initiated by a war cry. Hand-to-hand fighting then took place, the main weapon being a stone-headed war club – the outcome was generally brief and bloody. Territory was thus gained, together with loot, trophies and scalps.

An alternative strategy, and one most preferred, was for a large war-party to locate a small, isolated enemy camp, creep up on it during the night and make a surprise attack at dawn, slaughtering the inhabitants. As Saukamappee put it: "The great mischief of war then, was as now, by attacking and destroying small camps of ten to thirty tents, which are obliged to separate for hunting..."[25] The outcome was not much different to the ancient warfare on the Missouri River, where archaeological evidence indicates entire villages might be destroyed.[26]

Archaeological evidence and early engravings – such as that of the Delaware village in Sasquesahanok (p. 93) – prove that many settled communities in the eastern part of North America commonly fortified their villages. Generally, there was a protective palisaded wall of upright wooden poles, bound together with rawhide or roping. This enclosed the bark longhouses which surrounded a central square or plaza. Outside the palisade were cleared areas for growing crops.

Below: *Crow shields, both dating from the early nineteenth century. Examples of spiritual and mechanical protection: The shield of Rotten Belly, a distinguished chief of the Mountain Crow (Left). The shield of Shot-in-the-Hand, made of buffalo hide and embellished with the feathers and a head of a Canada goose (Right).*

Such arrangements were replicated as far west as the Missouri River: thus, the early Huff site, a Mandan village which dates from circa 1500 (and is still to be seen some eighteen miles southeast of the town of Mandan in present-day North Dakota), encloses an area of about seventeen acres. The fortifications were complex, consisting not only of a high, fort-like palisade but with bastions at the corners, a deep, wide surrounding ditch and a type of *chevaux de frise* of sharpened stakes. Defensive fortifications of this type indicate concern for protection from outside groups and it is reasonable to suppose that this show of force was matched by an increase in group solidarity.[27]

Such fortifications were obviously not used by nomadic Plains groups, as Lt. James Bradley observed of the Blackfeet (and which, he said, extended to other Plains tribes), "[they] never fortified their camps, and it was rare that they chose them with any reference to their possibilities of defense..."[28] As Ewers observed, Plains Indians, it seems, relied very heavily upon their dogs to bark and waken them "if enemy raiders entered the camp at night."[29]

Horse corrals, however, were commonly used by the Plains and Plateau tribes. Lowie[30] refers to the Northern Shoshone keeping their horses **inside** their camp circles, which implies a form of corral being used similar to that described for the Crow who, it is reported, made corrals of brush piled between the lodges to enclose the centre of the camp.[31]

Horses corralled this way, in the centre of a Flathead tipi village, are illustrated on p. 94. The episode recorded here suggests that it was not always an effective way of preventing loss of good horses to a determined horse thief!

Warfare tactics in the Northeastern Woodlands
Similar methods of pedestrian warfare to those described by

Above: *Plains Indian shield, Crow (?), circa 1850. Some 19 inches (0.5m) in diameter, the shield has several covers, each embellished with protective paintings, perhaps to match the situation. The symbols appear to make reference to sky and bear powers – highly significant to the Crow.*

Right: *A Mescalero Apache chief, photographed circa 1885. As shown here, the shields of this Athapaskan-speaking Southwestern group frequently display abstract and striking paintings. Generally, the designs make reference to the mountains and the spirits which dwelt there – (Gan), lightning, wind, snakes and the stars and planets. Shields such as these were carried by high-ranking leaders whose powers had been obtained from the supernatural world of the Apache people.*

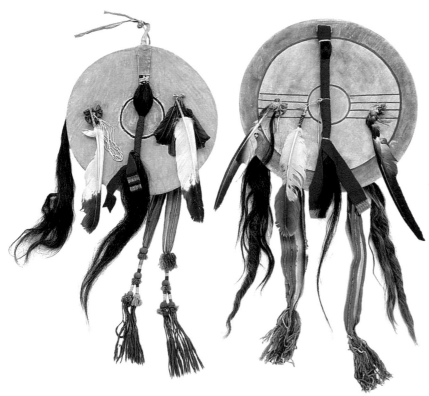

Far left: *Model of a Kiowa shield collected (1891–1904) by the ethnologist, James Mooney, as part of a project relating to Plains Indian heraldry. This is the shield design of* Padalti, *grandson of* Dohasan, *and head chief of the Kiowa until his death in 1866.*

Left: *Model shield, design of* Tsonkiada, *a distinguished Kiowa warrior. Mooney's studies of Kiowa heraldry established a similarity in the overall appearance of their shields which was indicative of a close camaraderie. These warriors also wore similar body paint, observed the same ceremonial taboos and used the same war cries.*

Saukamappee for the Plateau and Plains, but modified by terrain constraints, also prevailed in the Great Lakes region and beyond. There are descriptions such as the use of body armor, large shields, shock weapons and the bow, but this ancient style of fighting rapidly went out of fashion with the introduction of the gun to the Woodlands early in the seventeenth century. As Secoy observed[32], warfare tactics were now organized not only by reference to a forest environment but markedly conditioned by the use of guns. Now it was more expedient to scatter forces, so allowing individual warriors to take best advantage of nearby cover – but still effectively support each other by fire. Thus, Woodland military tactics at this time maintained no regular formation; the warriors kept close enough together to support one another and, when hard pressed, retreated to the nearest available patch of woods where this style of warfare could be used to best advantage. Further, the shield and body armor, effective against the arrow and spear in earlier days but no longer a protection against the penetrating power of a bullet (as well as being cumbersome for rapid movement), were largely abandoned.

Although war tactics were similar throughout the Woodlands, some definite cultural separations did occur between the Eastern and Western groups. Specialized torture and cannibalism, which were a practice of both the Iroquois and the Huron[33], were virtually absent amongst the more Western Woodland peoples.

Tribes such as the Santee Sioux, who in the 1600s commonly both

Below: *The Delaware village of Fort Sasquesahanok, showing bark longhouses and the village fortified by use of a palisaded wall. Similar defenses were recorded for the Virginia Indians in 1585 and were also used by Missouri Indians as late as the 1880s.*

Above: *War lodge, probably Crow, circa 1880. This was photographed in the Montana wilderness by the author in 1993. These were the vital "headquarters" of war-parties.*

Left: *A Flathead campsite in the Rocky Mountains, as depicted by Sharp, a young Piegan artist in the 1890s. It shows an exploit of White Grass, who captured horses from within the tipi circle. Camp circles were not infrequently enclosed to corral horses at night.*

traded and warred with such tribes as the Ottawa and Huron, had a form of institutionalized crying as an honorable manner of greeting people. To the Eastern tribes, this was regarded as a "final loss of manhood and a weakness that they tried not to give way to, even under torture by the enemy.."[34] The Ottawa and Huron first regarded the Sioux as weak and cowardly; it was, however, a notion which later military conflicts "painfully contradicted."[35]

The impact of the horse on defensive weapon styles
The ancestor of the horse probably originated in the Americas over forty million years ago. It was then a relatively small creature and there is no evidence that it was ever domesticated by the ancestors of the American Indian – rather, it was hunted and eaten. The creature, however, dispersed to the Old World via the land bridge to Siberia, eventually reaching Europe and disappearing in the Americas.[36]

Some ten thousand years or so later, after the horse had been reintroduced to North America, it was the Spanish stock-raising settlements in the Southwest which became the major source of horses for the Southern Plains tribes, notably the Comanche. By the early 1700s, a combination of trade, raids and wild horse herds led to a gradual movement northwards of a creature which radically changed the lifestyle of the indigenous population – not least, warfare tactics.

As the horse spread northwards from the Southern Plains to the Plateau, tribes such as the Shoshone, Nez Perce, Coeur d'Alêne and Kutenai in turn traded them – by a complexity of links to the Crow, Blackfeet and later to the Upper Missouri Village tribes.

Equestrian travel demanded freer use of arms and legs and this led to a modification of weaponry, not least that used for defence, and there were great changes. The late eighteenth century equestrian tribes, such as the Yankton Sioux, were now wearing an attenuated multilayered garment with sleeves which extended only to the elbows, and they carried smaller shields. The main reason for this, was that the foes of the Sioux to the west and south "still lacked guns, and hence used bows during this early period, so that these elements of the leather armor complex still had defensive value in battle against them."[37] Other styles of attenuated armor which could be worn on horseback were also used by such tribes as the Shoshone, Blackfeet and Plains Apache; these were sleeveless, some being painted red, green or blue. The garments must have looked similar to that worn by the Tonkawa warrior sketched by Lino Tapia in Texas in 1829 (p. 88).

Horse armor

Although, as discussed earlier, there is still some debate regarding the possible influence of the Spaniards on indigenous American warrior protective armor styles, there seems little doubt that the use of horse armor was an idea introduced from Europe.[38]

Below: *Comanche warriors sketched by George Catlin, 1834. Such scenes depicted the great skills of the Comanche in handling horses. Here, in a sham battle, a horse is being used as a shield – a dangerous feat seldom used in actual warfare.*

Right: *A shield said to have belonged to the Oglala Sioux war chief, Crazy Horse. Some 22 inches (60cm) in diameter, it was captured by Lieutenant Henry Lawton in 1877. The general layout of the design conforms to Wissler's informant's description of traditional Sioux shields and evokes several desired protective powers of fleetness and strength (Wissler, 1907). Some symbols, however, such as the red and black power motifs (extreme left), are decidedly Cheyenne. Crazy Horse was a close associate of the Cheyenne Dog Soldiers.*

The use of horse armor by the Shoshone was commented on by Lewis and Clark in 1805, who observed: "They have a kind of armor something like a coat of mail, which is formed by a great many folds of dressed antelope-skins, united by means of a mixture of glue and sand. With this they cover their own bodies **and those of their horse** [author's stress], and find it impervious to the arrow."[39] This type of horse armor had a much more limited distribution amongst the horse-using tribes in the Southwest, Plateau and Plains. It appears not to have spread very far beyond those tribes who were in close contact with the Spanish and seems seldom employed by tribes on the Central and Northern Plains – probably because of the relatively early introduction of the gun into these regions, which would render such armor virtually useless. As with the warshirt, however, the armor tradition was retained with the adoption of single-layered horse

Above: *Pictograph by the Hunkpapa Sioux leader, Sitting Bull, circa 1880. This probably shows an episode in the killing of the mail carrier, MacDonald, near Fort Totten in 1868. The shield carried by Sitting Bull brings together a number of elements in a single circle of defensive, protective and supernatural powers of the Sioux cosmos.*

masks and caparisons – now adorning, rather than protecting, the horse.[40]

Another style of horse armor was also in vogue on the Plateau and Central and Northern Plains, and it differed considerably from the Spanish type. It was made of a single layer of thin, white/yellow rawhide and exhibited four shield-like discs, often elaborately decorated (p. 85). It is certain that these date from at least 1820, but were still used by the Crow in dress parades as late as 1910; the evidence suggests that such coverings put more emphasis on protection of the horse by the symbolic designs, rather than the mechanical protection of the rawhide.[41]

Shields carried by equestrian warriors

Large shields were unwieldy on horseback and not popular – although there were notable exceptions, particularly on the Southern Plains.

Large shields were still popular amongst the Southern Plains tribes as late as the 1830s, even though tribes such as the Comanche had been equestrians for more than a century. Paintings by Catlin[42] and Berlandier[43] confirm the use of shields 3 feet (90cm) or more in diameter. Possibly, as with the lance, it was the influence of the Spanish which encouraged the retention of shield styles, although the actual method of construction differed. Thus, Pfefferkorn[44] described the Spanish soldiers' shields for the mid-nineteenth century as "egg shaped" and being made of several layers of rawhide which were riveted together. In contrast, most Plains shields were circular and generally of a single unreinforced thickness of buffalo rawhide. There were, however, exceptions to this and again the idea was possibly due

Right: *Pictograph on a buffalo robe, probably Cheyenne, circa 1860. Recent research (Cowdrey 1995) suggests that the horn-like hair-style identifies the individual as of Suhtaio descent – a tribe that merged with the Cheyenne in the early nineteenth century. The shield conforms to known Cheyenne styles (Nagy, 1994). Note the two Thunderbird-type motifs attached to the shield.*

99

to Spanish influence. It has been reported that one style of shield favored by the Comanche was the use of two discs of rawhide which were laced together around the edge of a wooden hoop. The space between the discs was then packed with hair, feathers, grass or other material, to reduce the momentum of the impinging missile. One can only speculate as to the effectiveness of such shield styles from the ball

of a muzzle-loading flintlock; however, there was a demand for suitable packing material by the Comanche. Anglo-American pioneers, it has been reported, were puzzled by the Comanche's apparent **sudden** interest in books. The dichotomy was later explained after a Comanche shield was captured in battle – it was found that, instead of the usual packing material between the rawhide layers, there were scores of pages from a book dealing with the complete history of Rome![45]

It is obvious that early observers were impressed with techniques of shield production. Catlin, for example, described the elaborate ceremonial of "smoking the shield," which he thought was "very curious, as well as an important one... For this purpose a young man about to construct him a shield, digs a hole of two feet in depth, in the ground, and as large in diameter as he designs to make his shield. In this he builds a fire, and over it, a few inches higher than the ground, he stretches the rawhide horizontally over the fire, with little pegs driven through holes made near the edges of the skin. This skin is at

Left: *White Horse, a noted Kiowa chief and war leader, photographed shortly before his death in 1892. He holds his famous cow shield which exhibits stylised renderings of the powerful and aggressive longhorn which the Kiowa viewed with awe, valuing it highly as a source of supernatural power. White Horse carried this shield in successful battles against both Navajos and Texans prior to 1875. It was one of the last available shields known to have been used by a prominent Kiowa leader.*

first, twice as large as the size of the required shield; but having got his particular and best friends (who are invited on the occasion), into a ring, to dance and sing around it, and solicit the Great Spirit to instil into it the power to protect him harmless against his enemies, he spreads over it the glue, which is rubbed and dried in, as the skin is heated; and a second busily drives other and other pegs, inside of those in the ground, as they are gradually giving way and being pulled up by the contraction of the skin. By this curious process, which is most dexterously done, the skin is kept tight whilst it contracts to one-half of its size, taking up the glue and increasing in thickness until it is rendered as thick and hard as required (and his friends have pleaded long enough to make it arrow, and almost ball proof), when the dance ceases, and the fire is put out. When it is cooled and cut into the shape that he desires, it is often painted with his *medicine* or *totem* upon it …"[46]

Catlin, as well as others, reported on one of the important aspects of many shields which are the symbolic designs which were considered to give supernatural protection to the owners; there was also much ceremonial, in their production,[47] and often associated ritual and taboos, such as with the famous shield owned by the Crow chief, Rotten Belly (p. 89). For these reasons, it is recorded, white traders were entirely unsuccessful in their attempts to introduce polished metal shields to the Blackfeet,[48] and they were certainly never adopted by any other equestrian tribes. Very elaborate and highly symbolic shield designs were a characteristic of some Apache, as well as Pueblo, groups (p. 91).[49] Western Apache shields are described as imbued with great protective and concealing powers and could only be made by men with knowledge of the appropriate "power."[50] (See Chapter V: Symbolic Weapons). Such elaborate shields were matched on the Plains by the Kiowa and Kiowa Apache and so intrigued the anthropologist, James Mooney, that he attempted (but never completed) a detailed study of Plains Indian Heraldry.[51] For the two tribes, he identified some fifty (painted) shield patterns and recorded that all the warriors carrying shields constituted a close brotherhood, with similar war cries, body paint and ceremonial taboos and regulations – sentiments which could surely be echoed for most of the warrior fraternities throughout North America from time immemorial.

CHAPTER FIVE

Symbolic Weapons

*"In all of these conceptions we find less appeal for the direct
destruction of enemies than for a shielding protection to enable
the man himself to be the destructive agent."*[1]

Above: *This pair of Magic Horns
was worn by a Northern Cheyenne
warrior in both the Battle of the
Big Bend of the Rosebud, June 17,
1876, and in the Custer Battle on
the Little Bighorn River, June 25,
1876. The horns were devised by
the medicine men of the tribe and a
warrior wearing a pair of these was
believed to be bulletproof.*

Right: *Choctaw ball game. Referred
to as "Ish ta boli", the game was
described as "The Little Brother of
War" – many pre- and after- game
ceremonials resembling those used
on the warpath. George Caitlin,
who painted this scene in 1834,
recorded that there were "almost
superhuman struggles for the ball".*

INTERTRIBAL CONFLICT, extending over hundreds if not thousands of
years, had been a way of life for the American Indian.[2] The closing
of the frontier, however, in the late nineteenth century all but saw the
end of both defensive and aggressive warfare.

The ordinary physical training of young men – and occasionally
women – fitted them to endure the demands and hardships of the war

Below: *A pair of ballsticks collected from the Seminole by Alanson Skinner in 1910. The ball was caught and thrown with the two netted sticks. Closely resembling those used by other Southeastern tribes, the ballsticks have been likened to war clubs – symbolic weapons with the playing field compared with the battleground.*

trail and from the commencement of joining a war-party, the individual was obliged to discipline himself and to accept the various duties given by the leader. Only when the war-party was disbanded were these obligations considered fulfilled.

In most cultural areas, rank was gained by an individual's achievements and these were moderated by a complex system of ceremonials conducted by respected officials and society leaders. For example, war honors, nature of insignia, rank and status were sanctioned by the society in which the individual lived. At that time, war honors were public tokens of an individual's courage and ability. They were regarded as important credentials when considering that person's ability to perform a particular duty or hold a position of service or responsibility.[3]

Society ethos, relative to war, extended far beyond individuals. Thus, amongst such tribes as the Osage and the Omaha, there was a special ceremonial – the *Wate'gictu*, "the gathering together of facts accomplished," where war deeds were solemnized.[4] Keepers of the four Packs Sacred to War, reminded the men to state the truth, for the bird messengers contained within the packs (see p. 107), would report their deeds to Thunder, the God of War. For each of the honors he was to claim, and hence don the accepted insignia, a warrior

Below: *Sioux protective symbols, circa 1850. The man on horseback carries a long-stemmed pipe which identifies him as the leader of the war party depicted. The evocation of the bravery of the crane, the speed of a centipede and the death-dealing power of lightning are illustrated by the motifs on the warriors head and shield and the tail of the horse.*

103

Above: *An appeal to bear-power; a Blackfeet medicine man (1832) attempting to save the life of a wounded warrior. The great strength and tenacity of the bear – desirable qualities of any warrior – were widely recognized throughout North America.*

painted a small red stick which, when called upon to recite his deed before the assembled tribal members, was held above the Pack of War. At a given signal, he dropped the stick into the pack; if the deed had been disputed or the stick fell to the ground, it was believed that the man had not spoken honestly and "the man lost the honor he had sought to gain."[5]

The Keepers of the Sacred War Pack were themselves distinctively identified by elaborate tattooing, part of which made reference to the strength of the enemy who had been killed. Symbolically, their unexpended warrior days accrued to the War Pack Keeper (see also p. 107).

Such elaborate tattooing signified rank, status, achievement and power, and was an ancient and widespread custom used throughout North America.[6] Less permanent, often more personal, but still making powerful symbolic statements (particularly relating to warfare and often emphasizing protective symbolism), was the use of body and face paint. The use of symbols of protection and power in the form of painting was, in the case of the Plains Indians, extended to their horses. There is some evidence to suggest that the concept was extended to the embellishment of canoes by the Woodland and Northwest Coast tribes.[7]

Societal involvement matters relating to war extended to many tribes. For example, both the Iroquois and the Pawnee – more than a thousand miles to the west of the Iroquoian territory – subjected unfortunate captives to a number of horrendous ordeals[8] and, in the Pueblos of the Southwest, extensive religious rituals relating to departure on the warpath came under a complex and authoritative priesthood which was largely tribally elected.[9] Little wonder then that without the obligations of warfare and the associated ritual, ceremonial and society organization which went with it, most tribes found themselves in an anomic state – the old values no longer had any meaning and many of the conditions necessary for self-fulfilment and the attainment of happiness were no longer present.

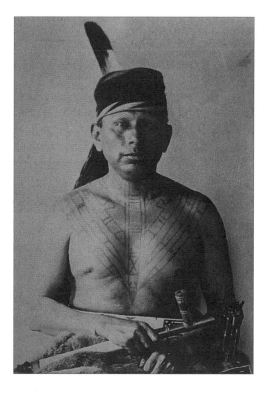

The war game

The losses accrued with the elimination of warfare also extended to the tangible manifestations of symbols of power, status, protection and achievement, which were so much the fabric of American Indian society. Their original meaning and values were largely lost and adjustments were made to accommodate the imposed changes. In the case of the Crow, where symbols of war achievement were no less important than with other Plains Indians, the cessation of intertribal warfare demanded that a new way had to be found to give young men the right to display the attainment of some type of warlike success; the solution was ingenious. In pre-reservation days, a warrior who had taken a gun from the enemy, or struck an enemy first, was entitled to wear a warshirt. Striking an enemy, considered the most important of the four major coups also, according to Crow informants, entitled the shirt-wearer to attach to the shirt, four quilled or beaded bands, one each over the shoulders and down the arms of the buckskin garment. Even as late as 1927, no Crow would publicly wear such a shirt unless he was entitled to it – it was a great distinction to be so adorned. The new, largely imposed, conditions were accommodated by warrior consensus and a new way was found "to give the ambitious youth the right to wear these shirts."[10] Thus, a number of young Crows, led by an older experienced man, offered a visiting Indian of a different tribe valuable gifts to persuade him to act as an enemy. The enemy, riding a good horse, then rode out from camp in the evening. Before dawn of the next day the Crows started on his trail and the individual who first managed to undertake and strike the first coup was then entitled to display the honors which were formerly earned by this act in actual

Above: *Star That Travels, Osage, 1897. He is tattooed with the "mark of honor", designating him as the Keeper of the Pack of War. The central tattoo represents a stone knife.*

Top: *A Crow war-pipe dating from the mid-nineteenth century. The pipe was smoked in ceremonial before battle as an appeal to the higher powers for success and protection.*

Above: Examples of face painting, Ojibwa, circa 1880. A wide range of face and body painting was used throughout North America in both war and peace ceremonial, much being distinctive to a particular occasion. Some, however, was more personal, the use and meaning acquired in a vision or vivid dream.

combat. There was, it seems, little "watering down" of the obligations because four times, and on different occasions, it was necessary for the same young Crow to "strike the first coup, which is usually done by hitting the "enemy" lightly with a stick or with the hand, before he is entitled to wear the decorated war shirt. This is one reason why they are valued very highly by the Crows..."[11]

The Little Brother of War

The change in tactics, while retaining much of the earlier symbolic war concepts as described for the Crow, was far from unique and, in fact, had parallels amongst the League of the Iroquois and other tribes, centuries earlier, in the ball game lacrosse. Played with a small ball of deerskin stuffed with moss or hair, or with a wooden ball, together with one or two netted rackets somewhat resembling tennis rackets (see p. 103), lacrosse was the favorite athletic game of most, if not all, the eastern tribes from the Hudson Bay to the gulf of Mexico.[12] The game could be, and often was, played on an almost tribal scale, with two settlements playing against each other and up to hundreds on each side. High stakes were wagered on the outcome.

As early as the 1630s, white missionaries such as the French Jesuit priest, Father François Joseph Le Mercier, reported on the obsession of the Huron with lacrosse – not only the game itself, but also its associated rituals and ceremonials, as well as the use of charms and talismans, some in the form of miniature lacrosse sticks. Obtained in dreams or ritual, these could be used to ensure success against the opposing team. The parallels to warfare are obvious; exhausting dance and song, fasting and finally the contest itself where the scoring posts could be miles apart, all point to the fact that many Southeastern tribes recognized that pent-up energies of virile young men needed demanding expenditure!

The ethos of the game was reinforced by the teachings of the distinguished prophet, Handsome Lake, a half brother of the Seneca, Chief Cornplanter. In the early summer of 1799, Handsome Lake experienced the first of a series of visions in which he received instructions from the Creator regarding future religious obligations of his people. He subsequently founded the Longhouse religion amongst

Above: *Osage medicine bundle, Ojibwa, circa 1880, referred to as a "waxobe". The bundles belonged to the Osage clans, the leaders of which directed the rituals associated with war and hunting. All contained a hawk skin which was used to rekindle the courage of the warriors who viewed it.*

Right: *There were a number of impressive shrines in the mountain regions of Zuni territory. This one, photographed in 1893, shows the carved wooden effigies of the Elder God of War which were located in the Twin Mountains, near the Peublo of Zuni in present-day New Mexico.*

Left: *Various decorated hats made of buckskin were worn by men of the Southwestern tribes; the two examples shown here were collected from the Navajo. The upper is embelished with owl feathers and abalone shells and the lower, which is of black buckskin, has two eagle feathers attached. The man is wearing a typical Western Apache hat of the type used in battle.*

Below: *A whistle made of eagle wing bone and decorated with ribbons and eagle feathers, Northern Plains, circa 1870. Such whistles were widely used on the battlefield. Here, war leaders signaled and directed warriors, the shrill note being clearly heard.*

the Iroquois. Its teachings expressly forbade violence and warfare and many former rituals connected with the warpath were forbidden.

Recent research reveals the similarities between lacrosse and warfare, almost certainly enhanced with the cessation of intertribal conflict and influence of Handsome Lake's teachings. Thus, in lacrosse, participants enter a world of "belief and magic, where players sewed inchworms into the innards of lacrosse balls and medicine men gazed at miniature lacrosse sticks to predict future events... bits of bat wings were twisted into a stick's netting... famous players were (and still are) buried with their sticks."[13] Likewise, the similarities between Ojibwa and Iroquois war clubs and elaborate versions of lacrosse sticks – for example, a clasped hand and dog image carved on an ancient Cayuga lacrosse stick – all point to an underlying ethos of war. "In the game we continue to wage war on our enemies" – a sort of secret emblem [which reinforced] the warfare/lacrosse analogy.[14]

Thus, a lacrosse stick, similar in shape to a drumstick and war club, and at times elaborately decorated to emphasize the relationship, was a symbolic weapon which signified the hidden ritual between game, music and warfare: the playing field was analogous to the battlefield. These conclusions are reinforced by a consideration of the way the Southeastern tribes referred to lacrosse – "brother to war" or the "little brother of war."[15]

War-pipes and war whistles

The earliest white travelers throughout North America repeatedly made reference to the custom of "fumigation of a peculiar kind"; it was a practice not easily understood by Europeans. In all important undertakings – as a compliment to visitors, before or during ceremonials, in the vision quest, prior to hunting or war – the pipe was smoked by all those present. When Cortés traveled through the Southwest in 1540–42, he was received with honor and "met" by persons carrying vessels with lighted coals to fumigate him.[16] In this region, amongst such tribes as the Hopi – but certainly not unique to them – smoke was always offered during ceremonials to the sacred powers; the pipe was handled with great reverence and care, an assistant attending the leader, ceremonial lighting of the pipe, transfer

Left: *A Lakota warbonnet made of eagle feathers, circa 1870. The use of feathers to signify war deeds and status was common in most cultural areas of North America. Eagle feathers were most coveted for the finest headdresses and were full of war symbolism. Ermine skin and buffalo horn embelishments evoked fleetness, courage and strength.*

Top right: *Details of an arrow, probably Mandan, circa 1830. The iron blade is sharp-edged and bound into the shaft with sinew, producing a formidable missile. The power of lightning is evoked by a channel engraved on the shaft.*

Middle right: *The spider web symbol worked in porcupine quills on a Lakota bag dating from circa 1880. Such designs were said by the Lakota to possess great protective power, embodying the observed fact that a spider's web is not destroyed by arrows or bullets – they simply pass through it, leaving only a hole.*

Bottom right: *A Diegueno shaman's wand which was used to "throw pain" into a tribal enemy. The wooden handle has a stone projectile point and is believed to date from before 1500 B.C. The Diegueno were a Yuman linguistic group of Southern California.*

in a set manner and offerings to the world quarters. Because of the remarkable similarity in the smoking customs throughout North America, it was recognized early on that the practice was of great antiquity and important to all undertakings, not least war.[17]

Pipe styles varied considerably. Amongst the Iroquois, a number were of wood and elaborately carved,[18] whilst those of many of the

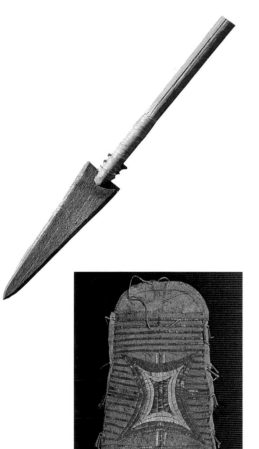

Plains tribes were of catlinite or black steatite.[19] Most commonly used, particularly in the east, was soapstone, the bowls frequently elaborately carved, the long stems embellished with quillwork, hair and feathers.[20] Associated pipe or tobacco bags were, particularly in early days, of complete otter or beaver pelts; later, they were of buckskin, quilled or beaded.

Most widely distributed was the "straight pipe," a simple tube of clay, chlorite, steatite, catlinite, or bone.[21] Of ancient origin, it was gradually replaced by the more elaborate styles but still retained in ceremonial and certainly, with a number of the Plains tribes, used on the war trail – hence the term "war-pipe". Of the war-pipe, the German scientist, Maximilian, commented in 1833: "The Indians on the Upper Missouri have another kind of tobacco pipe, the bowl of which is in the same line as the tube, and which they use only on their warlike expeditions. As the aperture of the pipe is more inclined downwards than usual, the fire can never be seen, so as to betray the smoker, who lies on the ground, and holds the pipe on one side."[22]

More specifically, Crow war leaders' medicine bundles contained tubular or straight pipes, either of catlinite or blackened stone, some accompanied with war effigies. Prior to battle, the consecrated pipe was ceremonially smoked, rituals performed, the effigies unwrapped and prayers made to the higher powers to evoke help and ensure success of the expedition. In this context, the pipe was a symbolic weapon. Such sentiments and ceremonials were widely recognized and used throughout North America from time immemorial.[23]

Of the war whistle, George Catlin noted that this was made of bone, ornamented with porcupine quills and carried by the leader into battle, "suspended generally from his neck, and worn under his dress."[24] Its practical use in battle was emphasized: when blown it was a sound that was "distinctly heard and understood... even in the

Below: *(Left)* Nesouaquoit *or "Bear in the Forks of a Tree", a Fox chief, circa 1840 in a poncho of bearskin. Whole skins were used to signify the powers of the animal, in this case the prowess of a grizzly. (Right) The Seminole chief Osceola (1833). Guns were adopted early by the tribes of eastern North America, some of whom thought at first that they possessed thunder powers.*

heat and noise... where all are barking and yelling.... the commands of their leader [would still be heard].[25] Similar descriptions of the use of the war whistle in battle have been made by other observers.[26]

The war whistle, generally made from an eagle wing bone, however, had a deeper symbolic meaning on the battlefield. In 1807, whilst mapping for the North West Company and traveling to the Upper Columbia and into present-day Idaho, the distinguished explorer, David Thompson, "the Astronomer," observed of his Indian companions: "Before daylight I set off with five Indians... This caused a halt, as we were surrounded and began to suspect that the enemy had planned to cut us off. The Indians put on their war-caps, uttering

some few words which I could not hear distinctly, and then began to whistle with a small bone instrument which they hung around their necks for that purpose."[27]

Years later, the anthropologist, Clark Wissler, drew attention to the fact that amongst all the Indians of the Plains, the thunder is usually associated with military exploits. Thunder was regarded as a bird – usually symbolized as an eagle. Eagle bone whistles generally had a zigzag line, usually in red, scratched down the sides (as representative of thunder power), and attached feathers of the yellow-winged woodpecker, a creature considered to be an associate of the Thunderbird.[28] The shrill tones from the whistle were considered to symbolize the cry of the eagle as representative of the Thunderbird and, as Wissler put it, "In battle, or sometimes in stress of great trial, they are sounded to call up the power of the thunder to rescue the unfortunate one."[29] Thus, attack or retreat in battle, the shrill of the eagle bone whistle[30] was more than a mere mechanical action – it was also a call to the higher powers for help and protection to overcome the enemy.

Thunderbird concepts and images were, as with the pipe, widely and anciently used throughout North America. For example, as well as with the Plains Indians, tribes of the Northwest Coast did magnificent renderings in wood, tattoos and paintings of this mystical

Above: *A Lakota Ghost Dance shirt, circa 1890. Such garments were generally made of muslin but sinew sewn; they were elaborately painted with symbols which appealed to the higher powers for protection. The blue is symbolic of "Taku Skan-skan", the energy or moving force of the Lakota universe. Motifs representing hail and lightning evoke the thunder powers.*

113

creature (see p. 118) and the Eastern Woodland people from the Winnebago to the Iroquois embellished regalia – particularly bags and pouches – with motifs of the Thunderbird in quill or beadwork. Often associated with underwater mythical beings, much of the symbolic ethos was associated with warlike activities and an appeal to the supernaturals for help and protection.[31]

War shrines and war packs

Many indigenous settlements throughout North America had a plaza for gatherings, most of which contained a central shrine or pole, as symbolic of village unity. The concept was obviously ancient – watercolors produced in 1585 by the Englishman, John White, of the "towns" of Secoton and Pomeiooc of the North Carolina Algonquians, show these features.[32] Westward, to tribes such as the Mandan on the Missouri River, there are very similar descriptions and illustrations, particularly in the 1830s, of a central and highly symbolic shrine.[33]

Likewise, in the Southwest – although shrines were generally in more secluded places – such as with the Zuni[34] where the War Gods are important deities and are the patrons of the Bow Priest cult whose duty it is to keep the scalps taken in war and the associated war fetishes.[35] Complex ceremonials associated with such Gods ensured protection from evil forces. A similar ethos permeated through the Pueblos and camps of the Southwest in a complexity of ritual and ceremonial and there were strong associations with Thunder and Sky powers (such as the Morning Star) – religious concepts associated with war which had many parallels in other cultural areas.[36]

Amongst one of the best descriptions of the need of a community unity by such shrines has come from the classic studies of the Omaha and Ponca tribes by Alice Fletcher and Francis La Flesche.[37] Here, both the sacred pole and cedar pole had anciently served for aeons as a symbol of provider, protector and source of spiritual power to the people. The warlike association was underlined by a close link with the Tent of War, War Packs and, as mentioned earlier, the tattooing of the honorary keeper.[38]

The poles were closely associated with the thunder, ancient mythology making reference to the Thunderbirds as envoys of the

Above: *Pictograph of a Lakota warrior in battle drawn by Little Big Man. This possibly depicts the war leader, Crazy Horse, wearing a warshirt which is embelished with eagle feathers and lightning symbols – a sign of his rank and an appeal to the thnder for aid in overcoming the enemy.*

Thunder Gods and endowing them with supernatural powers. "As a result," the Legend says, "the people began to pray to the Pole for courage and for trophies in war and their prayers were answered." [39]

> Te'xi ehe gthito^{n}ba
> Wagthito^{n}bi, wagthito^{n}bi, te'xi ehe gthito^{n}ba
> (Their Sacred, Sacred Pole,
> With reverent hands, I say, they touch the Sacred Pole before thee)
> (PART RITUAL SONG. OMAHA)[40]

The gun

As discussed, the power of the thunder and lightning was viewed with awe in most cultural areas; symbols of Thunderbird, lightning and associated spirits such as the underwater monsters were replete on much religious and military regalia and accoutrements. Little wonder that the gun had great impact on those tribes who first encountered its use. The defeat of the Mohawk in 1609 at Ticonderoga by a combined force of Huron, Montagnais and Ottawa (with the help of arquebus-armed French under Samuel de Champlain) forcibly

Right: *"Testing the powers of the Ghost shirt." The use of symbols for spiritual protection is nowhere better illustrated than by the painted and embelished garments once worn tribes such as the Sioux and Arapaho when the Ghost Dance religion swept the Plains in the late nineteenth century.*

demonstrated the **practical** advantages of gunpowder over native weaponry. But it was more than this: there is good evidence which suggests that this curious hollow rod, which made such a thunderous noise when a little lever was pulled and which hurled a missile so swiftly that it was impossible to even see it fly (and caused such havoc in its wake), inspired terror and awe in the minds of most of the Indian people. As Nicholas Perrot observed in the late 1600s, the "guns so astonished" the Indians of the Lake Superior region that they declared "there was a spirit within the gun, which caused the loud noise made when it was fired".[41] Later, he reported that when the Sioux visited the Ottawa and witnessed their firing of some guns, the report of these weapons so terrified the Sioux that they said it was the thunder or the lightning of which the Ottawas had made themselves master "in order to exterminate whomsoever they would."[42] Other references in the literature describe the panic created when guns were used and often, it seems, it was the noise and smoke which did more harm than the bullets. As the ethnologist John C. Ewers observed, "Indians gained a respect for the old muzzle-loading, smoothbore

Above: *A painted shield cover circa 1850. Although unidentified, it is probably Cheyenne. The horns appear to be giving protection from missiles in flight toward the wearer.*

Left: *Pictograph, probably Cheyenne, collected by the Englishman William Blackmore on the Platte River in 1874. The wounded warrior on the left carries a bow-spear and is wearing a buffalo horn headdress. "Buffalo Power" was particularly important in Cheyenne religion and protective symbolism.*

trade musket which was out of all proportion to its effectiveness as a lethal instrument."[43]

Of interest is that even after the tribes owned a considerable number of guns, some of them attributed their success or failure in the use of these weapons, to medicine power rather than their abilities as marksmen. Thus, when the French trader, François Larocque, met a party of well armed Crow Indians in the summer of 1805, their lack of success with their guns was attributed by the chief to the fact that "someone had thrown bad medicine on our guns and that if he could know him he would surely die."[44]

Some thirty years later Maximilian, on visiting the Mandan and recording their complex and rich ceremonials and culture, was told of a Mandan ceremonial for consecrating firearms. There is little doubt that gun power was viewed as strong "medicine" and, certainly in early days, endowed with great spiritual offensive and defensive powers.

Below: *A crow shield dating from about 1840. The desire to utilize the protective powers of the bear is almost certainly the inspiration for the dominant red image painted on this shield. There are no missiles below the outstretched paw, suggesting protection of the vulnerable young.*

Animal protective powers

The likes of the regenerative powers of the apparently lifeless and tiny cocoon, the swift and mysterious dragonfly, the fragile spider web, and the flight of the kingfisher to the swift and resilient pronghorn, the wise and powerful buffalo and awesome bear – to name but a few – were woven into religious and military symbolism of the North American Indian. Special regalia and accoutrements such as buffalo horn and eagle feather headdresses (see p. 110), decoration with horsehair and plumes and pelts of various creatures, as well as elaborate shirts and mantles, evoked and appealed to these powers. For example, an early nineteenth century deerskin headdress – complete with ears and antlers – was described at the time of collection in the Great Lakes region as associated with shamanistic performance relating to hunting and warfare; the iconographic features "are the upper world motif of paired opposed double hooks and the red disk with a serrated edge... probably a representation of the sun manito."[45] Almost a century later, similar powers were being evoked with the complex designs on the so-called Ghost Dance shirts (see p. 113).

Nowhere are many of these concepts better illustrated than in the widely distributed bear symbolism. The strength, ferocity and great bravery of the bear, particularly the grizzly, were desired qualities of a warrior. Stylized images, often the paw, appear on costume and accoutrements such as on the regalia of *Nesouaquoit* (see p. 112), a high-ranking Fox (Prairie) chief who belonged to the Bear Society of his tribe. Bear paws, the complete hide (and often bear claws), all evoke or make references to the powers of this awesome animal.[46]

Likewise, the Plains Indians evoked bear power[47] for at least two purposes, treating the incapacitated and as war medicine. The artist, George Catlin, in the summer of 1832 near Fort Union on the Upper Missouri, depicted a Blackfeet Bear Medicine man performing rites over a wounded man (see p. 104).[48] Similar rituals were widely used

Left: *Haida rendering of a double Thunderbird. Symbolism associated with this mythical creature occurred in most of the cultural areas in North America. Generally viewed as a giant bird, the flapping of its wings produced the thunder and the flashing of its eyes, the lightning; the potential destructive power was held in awe. Impressive, often abstract depictions of the Thunderbird were, as shown here, produced by the tribes of the Northwest Coast, being indicative of rapport with this sky power.*

Right: *An early sketch (circa 1800) showing a returning Iroquois warparty carrying scalps and escorting a prisoner. The leader has two scalps on the staff, the one with longer hair indicating a male, the shorter hair, a female. The prisoner has a gourd rattle tied to his arm which would betray him should he try to escape. This prisoner is constrained by cords although some prisoner "ties" merely symbolized a subservient enemy.*

Top left: *Peace medal with image of Andrew Jackson, President of the United States. Made of bronze and generally and 4in (10cm) in diameter, the medals were given to prominet leaders, as a symbol of the peace and friendship desired by government officials in their dealings with, in the main, Woodland, Prairie and Plains tribes. The peace medal and the American flag were coveted and adopted by a number of tribes to demonstrate peaceful intentions and symbolically protect the community. As with many "spiritual powers" they were not always successful.*

PRISONERS OF THE IROQUOIS

by the Plains Indians which also extended into the Subarctic region and beyond.[49] Incised images of bear figures and bear tracks on widely scattered sites, both in the Rocky Mountains on the Great Plains and into the Woodlands region, suggest that the concepts of bear power were very widespread and ancient. One such petroglyph, it has been suggested, depicts the bestowal of supernatural power "upon a man by a bear."[50] In addition, necklaces of bear claws, as well as renderings of bear images in tipis, war clubs, in quillwork and beadwork, and the use of a bear jaw for the handle of a highly coveted stabber knife, all attest to the desire of Plains Indians to acquire bear powers.[51]

The supernatural protective power of the bear is nowhere more emphasized than on a shield (see p. 117) collected prior to 1841, from an Upper Missouri tribe (possibly Crow). Here, a large paw, painted in red and outlined in brown, dominates the design; it appears to be warding off enemy fire and protecting smaller bears – perhaps its offspring. These were situations often faced by the Plains warrior, particularly in the period of the Indian-White confrontation where warfare and attacks against village communities were a stark reality. Warriors not only needed to simply fight the enemy, but had also to protect their wives and children; under such circumstances, as in most cultural areas for time immemorial, a man needed to evoke additional spiritual help from the higher powers!

Endnotes

INTRODUCTION
1. Pohrt, 1986: 57

CHAPTER ONE
1. See particularly Peterson (1971: 4-6) for a detailed discussion of the terminology applied to axes, war clubs, hatchets and the so-called 'squaw axe'.
2. Brasser, 1961: 77.
3. For illustrations and detailed descriptions of war clubs and batons of the Northwest Coast tribes, see Arima and Dewhirst, 1990: 401.
4. Underhill also points out that such paddles were mainly used to anchor the canoes to the beach. (Underhill, 1945: 91).
5. Sturtevant and Taylor, 1991: 87.
6. Kroeber, 1904: 184.
7. W. C. Sturtevant (Washington, November 1999) drew my attention to the use of unusual carved wooden staves exhibiting this shape and used by the Creek as illustrated by Swanton (1922).
8. Champlain's explorations in Huron and Iroquois country in the period 1609–1616, are described in Goetzmann and Williams, 1992: 58–59.
9. Brunius, 1995: 158.
10. Brasser, 1978: 87.
11. At that time, Sweden also comprised Denmark and Norway.
12. The hafts of both of these clubs are decorated with wampum which, on the Copenhagen club, is more intact. The use of wampum to adorn tomahawks was recorded for the Virginia tribes as early as 1700. See Brunius, 1995: 156.
13. Although Brasser has dated both these clubs as 'probably pre-1650' (Brasser, 1978: 87), Brunius' subsequent researches establish that the earliest reference to the Stockholm specimen is 1686; the Copenhagen club was first documented in 1725 (Brunius, 1995: 157–158).
14. Brasser, 1961: 79.
15. In 1585, Thomas Hariot recorded that the tribes of the North Carolina coast used 'flat-edged wooden truncheons, which are about a yard long' (Brasser, 1961: 80).

16. Less than a decade ago the author collected a sword-type club from the Florida Seminole that is clearly related to this ancient weapon.
17. Brasser (1961) documents the description left by early explorers in the Southeast, such as Thomas Hariot (1585), Captain John Smith (1607) and Du Pratz (1758), who make reference to the use of a 'sword', 'scimitar' or 'halfmoon'-shaped clubs of wood, emphasizing the early use and importance of this style of weapon in the region.
18. Several of these tribes were moved west; some, like the Delaware moved to Texas as early as 1820 (Hodge, 1907: 385). The notched quirt appeared amongst the western tribes well before the mid-1800s. A piece collected by Duke Friedrich Paul Wilhelm of Württemberg and now in the British Museum, dates from this time. Of interest is the fact that it was probably collected in Texas from the Kiowa or Comanche (Gibbs, 1982: 59).
19. Lyford, 1945: 45.
20. Phillips, 1987: 86.
21. Brasser, 1961: 82.
22. (a) Feest (1983: 110–115) describes the distribution and early styles of this club. Amongst the earliest are those now in the Ashmolean Museum, Oxford.
(b) For a detailed discussion of those in the Swedish and Danish collections, see Brunius (1995: 159–163).
(c) I am indebted to Scott Meachem for this information (Woodlands Conference, British Museum, London, February 1999).
23. See for example: Phillips, 1984; Sturtevant, 1989; Bankes, 1999; and King, 1999.
24. Peterson, 1971: 88.
25. (a) Peterson describes and illustrates a fine specimen collected from the Teton Sioux about the middle of the nineteenth century, 'at which time it must have been relatively new' (ibid.).
(b) Certainly by the 1830s, some Middle Missouri tribes had the gunstock type club, as attested by Karl Bodmer's paintings of the

Arikara, *Pachtüwa-Chtä* at Fort Clark (Hunt, Gallagher and Orr, 1984: 283) and the Hidatsa, *Ahschüpsa Masihichsi* (ibid: 316).
26. This specimen is illustrated in Peterson, 1971: Plate 23. The three bowie-knife blades dating from circa 1850 are stamped on their ricassos with 'MANHATTAN/ CUTLRY (sic.) CCMP/SHEFFIELD'. Steel implements manufactured in England for the Fur Trade are discussed in Woodward (1965).
27. Lewis and Clark, Coues ed., 1893: 230.
28. ibid.
29. Peterson, 1971: 23.
(a) If the pictographic robe showing scenes of Mandan warfare (circa 1797) collected from the Mandan by Lewis and Clark is to be believed, several warriors are carrying the Missouri war axe in battle (See Ewers, 1957: Plate 1). The robe is now in the Peabody Museum at Harvard University.
(b) See also Fig. 16 of a pictograph by the Mandan chief, Four Bears, using a Missouri war axe in battle.
30. Excellent renderings of Missouri war axes being carried by distinguished warriors were made by Karl Bodmer at Fort Clark in 1834. See particularly Hunt, Gallagher and Orr, 1984: Plates 318 and 326.
31. Reproduced in American Anthropologist X. No. 1 (1910), 11. Additionally, Kurz sketched a warrior (Hidatsa?) carrying what appears to be a Missouri war axe and decorated with a fringed handle (Kurz, Hewitt ed., 1937: Plate 31).
32. Peterson, 1971: 23.
33. ibid: 26.
34. Other terms used to describe this style, were 'dagger bladed', 'diamond bladed' (ibid: 24).
35. Reportedly, the Mandans specifically requested the blacksmith of the Lewis and Clark expedition to make them such blades. I recall Ralph Williams of Culdesac, Idaho, showing me in 1977, two spontoon-type blades. These had been found at early Nez Perce burial sites. Mr. Williams then showed me Lewis and Clark's report on reaching the Nez

Perce in September 1805, where they found such tomahawks made by their own blacksmith at Fort Mandan – a few months earlier and some two thousand miles to the east! (For discussions of the complex and efficient Indian trade, see Taylor, 1984 and Swagerty, 1988).
36. Peterson, 1971: 26.
37. Holmes in Hodge ed., 1910: 773–774.
38. Feest, Macgregor ed., 1983: 113.
39. Pohrt discusses the confusion which has arisen regarding the use of the word 'tomahawk', pointing out that the term originally described a weapon of war. Some authors also applied the term to other native stone implements and wooden hand weapons. He offers a definition of the tomahawk: 'a weapon with a metal blade, usually iron or steel, hatchet-like in form, and designed or decorated in such a manner as to be distinguishable from a common hatchet. Tomahawks, whether undecorated or ornate, exhibit a refinement and finish not generally extended to the ordinary hatchet of the time' (Pohrt, 1986: 55–57).
40. Henry Timberlake In Peterson, 1971: 33. He also adds that the pipe tomahawk possessed the symbolic power of the mace for ceremonial functions.
41. Arthur Woodward's researches on the evolution and distribution of the tomahawk in North America, quotes a reference as early as the 1650s to the use of a metal tomahawk amongst the Indians in the vicinity of New York. (Woodward, 1946: 4).
42. Presentation pipe tomahawks which displayed superior craftsmanship and decorated with inlays of silver and occasionally gold were far more valuable. For a discussion of such styles, see Pohrt, 1986: 59–60.
43. (a) ibid: 57.
(b) The handle of a pipe tomahawk needs to be drilled for smoking; lacking the tools to bore a handle which could be two foot (60 cm) or more in length, Indians generally used ash; the pith could be burned

out with a hot wire. Or the handle could be split lengthwise, the pith removed, and the pieces glued back. Ash, as Pohrt has noted, was a favorite wood for pipe-stems where similar techniques were used.

44. I am indebted to the late Russell Robinson of the Royal Armouries, for generously giving me copies of his notes relating to trade goods. These he had researched at Beaver House, London, prior to the records being transferred to Canada in the late 1960s.

45. Pohrt, 1986: 57.

46. (a) The late Milford G. Chandler was one of the last skilled tomahawk makers, with an intimate knowledge of fabrication techniques learned from individuals who had directly made or had knowledge of the methods employed by agency blacksmiths (See Chandler in Peterson, 1971).

(b) The late Russell Robinson, who was Senior Armourer at the Tower of London, demonstrated to me almost forty years ago the various metal forging techniques which would have been identical to those employed by rural blacksmiths in North America. Some of Mr. Robinson's tools are still in the collections of the Royal Armouries.

CHAPTER TWO

1. (a) argillite – generally black and much favored by the Northwest Coast tribes; source was the deposits on Queen Charlotte Islands.

(b) catlinite – named after the artist and explorer, George Catlin – is mainly found in Minnesota. It was much favored for making pipes, but ceremonial-type objects, such as tomahawks and knives were also produced. Both argillite and catlinite were fine-grained, relatively soft when first quarried, but hardened on exposure; both could be polished.

2. Flint is classed as a variety of chalcedony; it originally referred to the materials found in the chalk beds of several European countries. The term has now been extended to include all those stones which are principally of a silica base. Impurities, and the original formation, give rise to a variety of colors and shades. An illustration of a number of chipped blades and points showing the beauty of the stone work is in Baldwin, 1997:2.

3. A photograph of this dance showing one participant carrying such a knife blade, is reproduced in Taylor, ed., 1994 (a)

4. Holmes in Hodge, ed.,1907–1910, Part I:718.

5. (a) Baldwin, 1997:2.

(b) A detailed discussion of flint knives and blades appears in Hothem, (1986), particularly Chapters I–VI.

6. Holmes has suggested that the manufacture of daggers of both copper and steel was modelled after both European and Asiatic patterns (Holmes in Hodge, ed.,1907–1910, Part I:375. The early style of *Dague a Rouelle*, carried in Nepal with the national sword (the Kora), resembles those made by the Northwest Coast tribes (See Stone, 1934:19).

7. Holmes in Hodge, ed., 1907–1910, Part I:346.

8. (a) Carver's encounters with both Chippewa and Sioux in the winter of 1766 were with bands in the region of Leech Lake and Belle Plaine (near the Blue Earth River in present-day Minnesota). (See Carver, Parker ed., 1976:90–102.)

(b) Hanson, 1975:11.

9. Hanson suggests that these knives were similar in some respects to the DAG or 'stabber knife', sold by the Hudson's Bay and North West Companies and supplied 'to nearly all the Canadian Indians and Eskimos' (ibid.). The DAG is discussed later in this chapter.

10. (a) Carver, Parker ed., 1976:97.

(b) Alfred Jacob Miller saw the Teton Sioux wearing neck knife sheaths some two generations later when he traveled to the Plains with Sir Drummond Stewart in 1833–1834 (Ross, 1968:79).

11. I have discussed this in some detail in Taylor, McCaskill ed., 1989:247. The triangular neck flaps of some Sioux shirts exhibit patterns worked in quill or beadwork which resemble the knife blade, perhaps even the handle (see p. 52 this chapter). This may indicate the particular status of the individual and relate to the early symbolism reported by Carver.

12. Morgan, White ed., 1959:175.

13. Bear Knife power was not, however, exclusive to the Blackfeet. John C. Ewers found that it prevailed amongst Siouan, Algonquian and Athapascan linguistic groups. The

Bear Knife was used by at least six tribes within these groups (See Ewers, 1968.Table I:143).

14. Wissler, 1912, Part I:134.

15. Gibson in Washburn ed., 1988:375.

16. The Tlingit, in particular, had access to iron prior to white contact, being the closest middlemen to sources of Asiatic iron. It was, however, considered a 'precious' commodity (ibid:376).

17. Together with the skins traded for glass beads, they were subsequently 'sold in Canton for £90... [all for] an investment of one shilling'! (See Lloyd and Anderson, 1959:21–22).

18. For a description of the Tlingit-style warfare – and the Northwest Coast tribes in general – see De Laguna, Suttles ed., 1990:215–216.

19. (a) Murray, Burpee ed., 1910:85

(b) As the temperature of metals decreases, the Modulus of Elasticity increases, so copper would be inclined to hold its edge at Arctic temperatures; iron and steel would become both hard and brittle.

20. Witthoft and Eyman in Krech, 1989:98.

21. An approximate 1% content of carbon in iron reduces dislocations and produces high grade steel suitable for knife blades, axes, and tomahawks. The high carbon steels may be hardened by heating and quenching in water/oil. The process could be carried out relatively easily by local blacksmiths or artisans.

22. Peterson, 1957:119.

23. Scalping was practised in North America prior to white contact (Owsley and Jantz, eds., 1994:335–343). It involved the removal of the Indian's scalp-lock or sometimes the entire scalp. It was not necessarily fatal (See Taylor, 1980:23 and 1997:21).

24. The Bowie knife – a fairly substantial knife with a straight blade, single-edged with a clipped point and possibly a false edge – was mainly produced in England by Wolstenholm and Rodgers & Sons, both of Sheffield. It was expensive and probably for this reason it found limited favor with American Indians. (See Coe, Connolly et al, 1989:108–112).

25. A trade knife of this type was collected by Sir George Simpson during his travels across Canada in the 1840s; it is now in the

Ethnographical collections of the British Museum, London (King,1982:92). See also Baldwin (1997:38) who illustrates a fine specimen which he dates at about 1800; it was made by Greaves and Sons of Sheffield.

26. The John Russell Company of Deerfield, Massachusetts, is still in business today.

27. Baldwin, 1997:56.

28. (a) See ibid:44 and 48 for observations and illustrations relating to the wide range of DAGS produced both in England and also by local American blacksmiths.

(b) DAGS hardly figured in the weaponry of the Teton Sioux (Hanson, 1975), emphasizing the Northern and Eastern distribution of the style.

29. See pp.42 and 53 for examples.

30. The technique of manufacturing such blades was demonstrated to me by the late Russell Robinson, Senior Armourer at The Royal Armouries, Tower of London, and an expert on metal-working. He used relatively simple tools to hand-forge the blades which seem to be mainly of mild steel (carbon content approximately 0.15% to 0.3%). He did not use case hardening.

31. Painter, 1992:36.

32. John Painter documents the location of similar knives (ibid:36–37). The associated Indian-made sheaths with these knives suggest a popularity with Cree and Metis groups and dating prior to 1850.

33. Peterson, 1957:121.

34. (a) See ibid. who illustrates such a sheath which is now in the Smithsonian Institution, Washington (specimen number 5417).

(b) See Taylor, Idiens et al., 1974:130.

35. Wissler, 1904:251 and Speck, 1928:5. Speck associates such knife sheaths with Oglala women. He also suggests that this was somewhat distinctive in Sioux arts and is [absent] 'in the bead ornamentation of knife-scabbards among other Plains tribes...' (ibid:6).

36. (a) Personal correspondence, Jim Hanson, Museum of the Fur Trade to C.F.T. August 10, 1999.

(b) See also Taylor, 1999 (In Press).

(c) As Hanson has observed, swords were sold to the tribes of the Eastern Woodlands as early as the seventeenth century. Although falling into disuse as weapons, they were 'symbols of rank for officers' (Hanson, 1975:45). Sword belts, embellished with quillwork, were produced by tribes such as the Iroquois (Brasser,1976:143).

37. McKenney and Hall, 1933, Vol.I:416.

38. Lowie, 1935:238.

39. See Galante, 1980 and Wildschut, Ewers ed., 1959 for further details on Crow sword and lance symbolism.

40. Galante, 1980:65.

41. Wildschut in ibid:67.

42. Cowdrey, 1995:19-20

CHAPTER THREE

1. Superbly shaped flintwork producing both spear and arrow heads is represented by such points as Clovis, Folsom and Eden, named after the locations in which they were found. Some date from more than thirteen thousand years ago (see Turner, 1979: 7).

2. Ewers, 1955: 201

3. An interesting comment by the Victorian ethnologist, Otis Mason, relating to tube projectile devices, was that the blow tube with the dart, driven to the mark by 'the elasticity of the breath, should be the antecedent and parent of the gun, pistol, and cannon'. He commented, however, that the inventors of gunpowder probably never saw an American or Malayan blow tube (Mason, 1894: 634).

4. Atlatl is an Aztec word for spear-thrower, a term now adopted by most American anthropologists. The Australian aborigines called them *woomera*. Spear-throwers were used throughout the world and Hamilton comments that they were 'in use in Asia and Europe for tens of thousands of years (Hamilton, 1982: 13).

5. Tate, 1986: 3.

6. These generally perforated stones are often referred to as 'banner stones' and were formerly thought to be totems or clan emblems. Simple physics calculations relating to effects on both momentum and kinetic energy of projectile with an atlatl suggest at least 4 to 5 fold increase in comparison without its use. A banner stone attachment would enhance this effect even more.

7. Garcilaso, 1951: 597.

8. Teit, Boas ed., 1930: 115.

9. Ewers, 1955: 201.

10. Pike, 1810: 10–11.

11. (a) A favorite point for lance heads in the historic period was a sword blade, which according to Dodge was 'procured in great number from the Mexicans' (Dodge, 1959: 421).
(b) An examination of lances in the reserve collections of the Smithsonian Institution (most from the Southern Plains) revealed that more than 70% had sabre blades as points. Several were clearly of high grade steel. (Discussions with John C. Ewers, Smithsonian Institution, Washington. August 1962, and studies at the S.I., October 1999).

12. Although the lance appears to have been used minimally in actual combat by the Central Plains tribes, a notable exception was the Hunkpapa leader, Sitting Bull, who favored the lance above all weapons. It was described as made of ash and 7 or 8 feet in length 2.1m - 2.4m, 'with an eight-inch notched iron blade' (Utley, 1993: 19).

13. (a) Hamilton, 1982: 26.
(b) Laubin's studies relating to the history of bow use in North America indicate that there was no evidence of its use by the earliest cliff dwellers, (circa 2000 B.C.), although 'it does show up in later ones'. He concludes that the North American bow seems 'to be of Asiatic origin but was brought over in later migrations, rather than in the early ones' (Laubin, 1980: 1).
(c) A recent paper by the scholar of American Indian archery, Roland Bohr, gives an earlier date than Hamilton and states that 'The oldest undisputed archery artifacts of North America date from about 500 A.D.' (Bohr, 1996: 2).

14. Laubin, 1980: 1.

15. Mason, 1894: 634.

16. ibid.

17. Hamilton, 1982: 29.

18. This was so named because it was taken from an Indian who was shot in Sudbury, Mass., in 1660.

19. Hamilton, 1982: 32,

20. Mason, 1894: 643.

21. Hamilton, 1982: 64.

22. (a) Mason, 1894: 638
(b) The geographical location of a tribe tended to largely dictate the type of wood used. Osage orange or *Bois d'arc* was widely recognized as amongst the hardest, finest and most

durable of timbers. It was straight-grained and ideally suited for bow making. The tree was plentiful along the Arkansas and Canadian Rivers, and in Texas. It was commonly used by the Comanche for their bows (Wallace and Hoebel, 1952: 100) and sought after in trade by other tribes. The Omaha referred to *Bois d'arc*, as 'yellow wood' and the Blackfeet called the tree itself 'smooth bow' but 'bow dark' seems to have emerged as a universal terminology (Taylor, 1975: 50).

23. Bohr, 1996: 4 and personal communication, February 1999.

24. Hamilton, 1982: 69.

25. The reflexing of a sinew-lined bow refers to the bow limbs sweeping backwards from the grip when the bow is relaxed (unstrung). To some extent this is due to the sinew-lining on the back of the bow. Such bows can reverse themselves in string during museum storage and errors are made as to which side the sinew was originally fastened. (See also ibid: 9 and 59).

26. Descriptions of ten horn bows in the United States National Museum were supplied to the scholar T. M. Hamilton, by Dr. W. R. Wedel. These had been made by George Metcalf, a meticulous technician at the museum. Mr. Metcalf made an error in thinking that some of the bows were of cow horn. Bill Holm's subsequent studies identified the material as mountain sheep horn (Holm to Taylor, 1992). These statistics are reproduced in ibid: 140–143).

27. (a) Ross, ed., 1968: 60.
(b) Miller took an interest in the horn bows used by warriors whom he saw practising with them at the Shoshone Rendezvous in 1833. He illustrated their target practise and made a sketch of a strung and unstrung horn bow (see DeVoto, 1948:Plate XLIX and ibid: 7).

28. Hamilton, 1982: 92–93.

29. Metcalf in ibid: 92.

30. Faris and Elmer, 1945: 161.

31. Hamilton, 1982: 89.

32. The string was one of the most important parts of the bow and required considerable skill in its manufacture. Most were made from the sinews of the deer, elk or buffalo; others, such as in the Southwest and sometimes in the Basin, were of twisted fiber. A disadvantage of

sinew was loss of elastic properties in conditions of high humidity. For this reason, most men carried a spare string and horn bows, in particular, were covered with a rattlesnake skin. (See Taylor, 1975: 51).

33. *Mahpiya Kinyeyapi*, 'Flying Cloud', (aka Judge F. B. Zahn), of Sioux descent and who lived at Fort Yates, N. Dakota – an excellent scholar who I corresponded with almost fifty years ago – reported that his old-time informants (such as Spotted Bear, aged 96 years) said that some Sioux bows were made of buffalo ribs, heavily backed with sinew. The bows were 'excellent' and were protected with a canvas cover 'so that rain or moisture would not soften the sinew and thus loosen the bows' splicing' (Zahn in Hamilton, 1982: 102).

34. (a) Several students of the American horn bow have made replicas and tested their properties (See Laubin, 1980: 77–78 and Holm in Hamilton, 1982: 116–134).
(b) The performances of bows collected from widely spaced tribes in North America were compared with those from other parts of the world – including a bow from the 'Mary Rose' which sank in Portsmouth Harbour in 1545. A replica of an English long bow of yew had a weight of 75 lbs. A sinew-backed Cheyenne bow had a weight of 80 lbs. The composite had a weight of 85 lbs. Bill Holm's second sheephorn bow was 39 inches (1.1m) long measured along the curve, with a weight of 55 lbs at full draw of 22 inches (0.55m) and maximum range 235 yards (212 metres). He found it difficult to hold at full draw and concluded that such bows were 'ordinarily drawn and shot in one motion'. Over a period of some twelve years, he reported that the reflex on the unstrung bow had increased (Personal communication, 1992). (See Pope, 1923 and Hamilton, 1982: 137–139. For the Holm references, see ibid: 120–123).

35. Ross, ed. 1968: 7.

36. As discussed in the main text, the material used for arrow shafts depended on the locality. Apache arrows were generally of easily obtainable straight marsh reeds with a heavy foreshaft of hard wood. The Apaches called the reed *klo-ka*, ('arrow grass') and the hard wood, *kk-ing.* Pawnee arrows were, according to Dunbar, an early observer of dogwood (*Cornus stolonifera*), those of the Shushwap were of service berry. Those of the Haida and Bella-Coola have been described as of cedar. (See Mason, 1894: 669, 674 and 676).

37. (a) Wilson, 1901: 527.
(b) Flint arrowheads could wound more than later metal ones. Skulls/ bones with flint arrowhead wounds have been found in prehistoric sites; in some cases the arrowpoints were very long, with drill-like characteristics (ibid: 517–518).

38. (a) ibid: 524–525.
(b) The weapons used – including trade guns – during the Indian/White confrontations, particularly in the second half of the nineteenth century are briefly covered in my earlier volume (Taylor 1975) which also gives further references.

39. ibid: 531.

40. Amongst the Mandan only a few individuals were taught to make arrows. The teachings were that those in need of arrows bought their supplies from them. Rituals were observed in the collecting of raw materials and the making the arrows. (See Bowers, 1950: 283).

41. Maximilian, Thwaites ed., 1906. Vol. 23: 354.

42. Care was taken to ensure that the shaft was straight. The 'arrow straightener' was a perforated bone, ivory or wooden device, which could be used in a lever-type mode to remove localized distortions. See p. 66 for an example from the Mandan which is typical of those used in several cultural regions.

43. The form of the feathers varied considerably. Sometimes they were used whole, as with many of the Eskimo groups and some of the Southwestern tribes. In other areas, the feather was split lengthwise. Feather length also varied; Plains arrows have long – up to 6 or 7 inches (15–18 cm) – fletching on a short shaft of hard wood. In the Southwest, the feathering was short on the long reed shafts with heavy foreshafts. Feathers were set on the shaftment, either flat or radially, secured with sinew at the ends. Sometimes, but not always, glued down. (See Mason, 1891 and 1894 for terminology and more details; Hough (1891: 62–63), who refers to

rifling techniques of the Pima; and Bourke (1891: 71–73), who discusses (with considerable authority) Apache arrows and fletching techniques of other tribes, such as the Pima and the Iroquois).

44. The Hudson's Bay Company lists arrowheads under Trade Goods offered at York Factory in 1813 – for trade to Canadian Indians. According to Garretson (1938: 180), hundreds of thousands were manufactured yearly by eastern traders to be exchanged for furs. They were put in packages of one dozen (costing six cents a package) and one package was exchanged for a buffalo robe. Some were also made by local blacksmiths and by the Indians themselves. A Sioux informant (White Hawk) said that arrowheads were frequently cut from 'thin frying pans sold by traders or used by the soldiers' (Densmore, 1918: 438). According to Wooden Leg, a few aged Cheyenne warriors continued to use flat arrowheads even as late as the 1870s. (Marquis T.B. 1957:73).

45. Holm 1981: 60.

CHAPTER FOUR

1. At first they traded with the Spanish but fighting soon broke out; a fleet of some eighty canoes attacked Ponce de León, compelling him to withdraw.

2. The Calusa practised human sacrifice of captives on a wholesale scale and were also cannibals. Subsequent further contacts with the French, English and other Spanish expeditions invariably ended in bloodshed and it took more than two centuries to subdue them. Most of the remnants – some three hundred and fifty souls – were removed to Havana.

3. (a) On occasions, such armor was adopted by the whites in their wars against hostile tribes. When fighting Indians around Chesapeake, Captain John Smith and his companions – at the suggestion of friendly Indians – protected themselves with a form of Massawomek armor which was made of 'small sticks woven betwixt strings of their hempe, but so firmly that no arrow can possibly pierce them' (Chamberlain In Hodge ed., 1907–10. Vol. I: 88). It was successful and the English 'securely beat back the Salvages (sic.) from off

the plaine without any hurt' (ibid.).
(b) As early as 1540, members of the Coronado expedition also adopted native armor. As Aiton recorded, 'The great majority wore native buckskin suits of armor, cueras de anta, which were much more comfortable on the march and quite effective against Indian weapons' (Aiton, 1939: 558–559).

4. Heidenreich, Trigger ed., 1978: 386.

5. The ivory plate armor of the Inuit and Eskimo peoples was believed by Boas to be an imitation of the iron armor of the Siberian Chukchi and he also commented that other styles of plate armor were of Japanese origin (Boas In Hodge ed., 1907 10. Vol. I: 88).

6. Leather body armor had intercontinental distribution in the Americas. A partially tailored multilayered buckskin garment in the British Museum (specimen number 1831, 4-16, 18), which was for years labelled as 'Plains Indian' and confounded several experts, was finally identified as from Patagonia (See Taylor, 1999). In style it is very similar to Lewis and Clark's description for the Shoshone in 1805 – as mentioned in the main text of this volume.

7. Ewers, 1955: 204.

8. Secoy, 1953: 74.

9. This particular shield from the Aleutian Islands is illustrated in Bancroft-Hunt, 1995: 195.

10. Teit, 1930: 117.

11. Ibid.

12. The Huron, a powerful tribe at the time, were first described by Jacques Cartier when he wintered at their village of Stadacona on the St. Lawrence river in 1535.

13. Hough, 1893: 631.

14. The Blackfeet alliance (which later included the Sarcee and Gros Ventre) with the Piegan at the forefront, entered the region of present-day Alberta and Montana in the mid-nineteenth century (Lewis, 1942: 13).

15. (a) Keyser, 1975: 213.
(b) The Blackfeet move to the Northern Plains was partially due to pressure from the gun-armed Cree to their east and, no doubt, to the possibility of obtaining horses from the western tribes.

16. Loendorf and Conner, 1993: 222.

17. McCoy, 1984: 5.

18. Hammond and Ray, 1953: 841.

19. Hotz, 1970: Plate 6.

20. Wissler (1910) and Lowie (1935).

21. I have considered the aspect of lunar and sky power designs on shields in an article to be published in *Patrick Moore's Year Book (2001) of Astronomy* (In Press). Additionally, the scholar Mike Cowdrey has considered some Crow shield designs and their lunar connections (Cowdrey, 1995 and personal correspondence).

22. Secoy, 1953: 35.

23. ibid.

24. ibid.

25. ibid.

26. Robarchek, Owsley and Jantz eds., 1994: 311.

27. Taylor, 1996: 17.

28. Bradley, 1923: 286.

29. Ewers, 1955: 207.

30. Lowie, 1908: 208.

31. Marquis, 1928: 149.

32. Secoy, 1953: 68.

33. Sturtevant and Taylor, 1991: 236.

34. Secoy, 1953: 65.

35. ibid: 66.

36. In 1493, Columbus brought the horse back to the Americas. It was a changed animal, selective breeding making it twice the size of the ancient wild horse, last seen in North America more than ten thousand years ago. It was largely the Spanish stock-raising settlements of the Southwest which became a source of horses to the Southern Plains tribes. By the early 1700s, a combination of trade, raids and the wild horse herds became the major source of horses for the Southern Plains tribes, notably the Comanche, who traded them to their kinsmen, the Shoshone.

37. Secoy, 1953: 74.

38. (a) Thus, some types of Spanish horse armor consisted of heavy leather covers for the entire body of the horse and covering the front, with apertures cut for the eyes. The overall style is reminiscent of the description by Lewis and Clark for the Shoshone (see main text).
(b) The Segesser I and Segesser II paintings, now in the Palace of the Governors in Santa Fe and which were discovered in Switzerland in 1945 (subsequently researched by the late Swiss scholar Gottfried Hotz), show depictions of this style of horse armor (Hotz, 1970: particularly Plates 5 and 6).

39. Lewis and Clark, Coues ed., 1893. Vol. 2: 561.
40. Taylor, 1944 (b): 123.
41. Taylor, 1995: 39–49.
42. See Taylor, 1994 (b): pp. 17 and 219.
43. Berlandier, Ewers ed., 1969: Plate 3.
44. Pfefferkorn, 1949: 291.
45. Wallace and Hoebel, 1952: 106.
46. Catlin, 1926: 271.
47. ibid: 271–272.
48. Ewers, 1955: 203.
49. Wright, 1976 and 1992: 44–51.
50. Ferg, 1987: 140.
51. McCoy, 1995: 64–71.

CHAPTER FIVE
1. Wissler, 1907:53.
2. See Owsley and Jantz, eds., 1994: particularly Chapter 24: 27–30.
3. Leading a war-party was a big responsibility and some of the best warriors cracked under the strain. Thus, one Kiowa war-party leader, *Tokuléidl*, who started out with a small company of about ten men, is reported to have 'apparently lapsed into some type of schizophrenic condition, obsessed with the delusion that all of his men were horses. On one day he stopped the party, lined up the warriors and examined the teeth of each man. Another day he forced all of them to bray in chorus threatening to shoot any man who did not bray or obey him or who deserted. The upshot was that the party was ambushed and practically exterminated' (Mishkin, 1940: 33).
4. Fletcher and La Flesche, 1911: 434.
5. ibid: 437.
6. (a) This is well illustrated in the case of the tribes of the Northwest Coast. Here, tattooing was practised by the higher classes being heraldic, totemic and, on occasions, personal crests of the wearers (see Taylor, 1997: 61 for illustrations of the Haida and a further discussion).
(b) Amongst the Omaha, a warrior who had won war honors in battle was entitled to tattoo his body or that of his wife or daughter as a mark of distinction. The tattooing was done by an expert in the rituals connected with the ceremony. The needles used had the rattles of the rattlesnake attached (see Fletcher and La Flesche, 1911: 221).
(c) For a discussion of the tattooing practises of the Cree and other

northern tribes, see Light, 1972.
7. (a) See Sturtevant and Taylor, 1991: 112 and 170.
(b) See also Adney and Chapelle, 1964: the reference to a Passamaquoddy war canoe motif (p. 82).
8. (a) Sturtevant and Taylor, 1991: 236 (Iroquois) and Taylor, 1994 (b): 67–74 (Pawnee).
(b) See also Seaver, 1982: 103–115.
9. See, for example, Hoebel, Ortiz, ed., 1979: 414 (Zia Pueblo) and Ladd, Ortiz ed., 1979: 488 (Zuni) for reference to the place of the religious leaders in war matters.
10. Wildschut, Ewers ed., 1960: 38.
11. ibid.
12. Culin refers to Lacrosse as Racket and emphasizes that it was mainly a man's game. Shinny, he reports, was 'especially a woman's game' and it was 'frequently referred to in the myths' (Culin, 1907: 562 and 616–617).
13. Vennum, Jr., 1994: xv.
14. ibid: xiv.
15. ibid: 213.
16. McGuire in Hodge ed., Vol. 2, 1910: 603.
17. McGuire emphasizes that 'Every individual engaging in war, hunting, fishing, or husbandry… made supplication to the gods by means of smoke, which was believed to bring good and to arrest evil [and] to give protection from enemies…' (McGuire in ibid: 604).
18. King, 1977: Plates 1–14.
19. For a discussion of the stone, catlinite, see Catlin, 1926, Vol. II: 233–234 and for black steatite, see Ewers, 1963: 45 who refers to the best type of 'calcareous shale'. This was found at Pipestone Cliff on the south side of the Two Medicine River in present-day Montana.
20. In 1540, Alarcon found the Indians on the lower Colorado River employing 'small reeds for making perfume' and likened them to 'the Indian *tobagos* of New Spain' (McGuire in Hodge ed., Vol. 2, 1910: 603).
21. A Blackfeet drawing of a straight pipe is reproduced in Wissler, 1912: 170–171). This had been taken from a Beaver Bundle of ancient origin. Straight pipes, according to Ewers' informant, Green-Grass-Bull, were considered 'very holy object[s]' and were used in the oath of swearing 'by the pipe'. A straight pipe specifically

associated with war medicine and with the Blackfeet Catcher's Society Pipe Bundle, has also been documented by Ewers (1963: 36–37).
22. Maximilian in ibid: 38.
23. The complexities of pipe rituals is well illustrated with the ceremonial manner of smoking the Sacred Pipes during council deliberations of the Omaha Seven Chiefs Society (Fletcher and La Flesche, 1911: 207–209).
24. Catlin, 1926, Vol. I: 273.
25. ibid.
26. The use of the war whistle by the Comanche and Cheyenne is discussed by Ewers (Berlandier, Ewers, ed., 1969: 176).
27. Thompson in Wissler, 1907: 47.
28. Wissler reports that his Dakota informants said that before a storm, the yellow-winged woodpecker gave 'a peculiar shrill call not unlike the sound [of the eagle bone war whistle]' (Wissler, 1907: 47).
29. (a) ibid.
(b) Wissler said that the U.S. emblem of the eagle with outstretched claws, holding arrows and the lightning, was regarded by the Dakota 'as an appeal on our part to the thunder-bird' and that 'statements to the contrary are usually interpreted as white men's lies to deceive the Indians and to guard the power' (ibid: 48).
30. Berlandier, Ewers ed., 1969: 176.
31. Phillips, 1984: 42–43.
32. Hulton, 1984: Figs. 24 and 35.
33. Such shrines evoked protective symbolism with the Mandan. See Taylor, 1996: 66.
34. It was, however, the Deer and Bear clans who performed the public ceremonies for the War Gods (see Ladd, Ortiz, ed., 1979: 488).
35. Acoma mythology refers to the weapons of war being given to young warriors by the Sun (see Parmentier, Ortiz ed., 1979: 615).
36. (a) On a more personal level, Kachina dances were sponsored by the ill person or his family to help in curing (see Stanislawski, 1979: 598).
(b) See Taylor, 1994(a): 44–45 (Thunder and sky powers of the Plains tribes): ibid: 91 (Sky powers of the Northwest Coast tribes): ibid: 115 (The Arctic).
37. Fletcher and La Flesche, 1911.
38. This also extended to hunting rituals. The ancient Cedar Pole, (preserved in the Tent of War) stood

adjacent to the tent which housed the White Buffalo Hide, associated with buffalo hunting (ibid: 229).
39. (a) ibid.
(b) The complexities of the ceremonials and mythology relating to the Sacred Pole are recorded in ibid: 245–251.
40. ibid: 233–234.
41. Ewers, 1967: 38.
42. ibid.
43. ibid.
44. ibid:39.
45. Phillips, 1984: 51.
46. Not all cultural areas held the gun in such awe. As Bill Holm has observed, 'Guns came into very early use [on the Northwest Coast]. I don't think they were ever rated *wakan*. Most NWC tribes had traditions of a death bringer, which was easily related to the gun, and seemed almost familiar. Vancouver's men shot a seagull on the wing to impress local Puget Sound viewers, who responded with "poo poo" as if inviting them to do it again! Vancouver found every canoe at the Nimkish village armed with a gun (the chief owned 8 muskets!) and they had never before seen a white man! There are a number of accounts of trading guns…' (Holm to CFT, personal correspondence. April 18, 1999).
47. Bear power for the Northeast is well illustrated in the photograph of Keokuk and his son, Moses Keokuk (see Sturtevant and Taylor, 1991: 245). Both wear magnificent bear claw necklaces. That of Moses is now in the National Museum of Denmark, Copenhagen (catalogue number Hc397).
48. George Catlin described this man's costume in great detail (Catlin, 1926. Vol. 1: 46). Ewers reported that the Plains Indians who acquired bear power not only used it to treat the sick and wounded, but also as war medicine (Ewers, 1982: 38).
49. Ewers, 1968: 144-145.
50. Ewers, 1982: 38.
51. The artist DeCost Smith reports his conversation with *Topompy*, chief of the Lemhi Shoshone. *Topompy* refers to warriors being 'friends with bears' and communication with bears 'in a dream' (Smith, 1943: 120–121). A painted buffalo robe, identified as Sioux, depicts a bear 'as a source of a successful war party leader's power' (Ewers, 1982: 42).

Bibliography

Adney, Edwin Tappan and Howard I. Chapelle *The Bark Canoes & Skin Boats of North America*. Washington: Museum of History & Technology, Smithsonian Institution. 1964.

Aiton, Arthur S. Coronado's muster roll. *Amer.Hist.Rev,* Vol. 44, No.3: 556–570. 1939.

Arima, Eugene and John Dewhirst. Nootkans of Vancouver Island in *Handbook of North American Indians,* Vol.7 Northwest Coast: 391–411. Ed. Wayne Suttles. Washington: Smithsonian Institution. 1990.

Baldwin, John *Early Knives and Beaded Sheaths of the American Frontier.* West Olive, Michigan: Early American Artistry-Trading Company. 1997.

Bancroft-Hunt, Norman *Warriors: Warfare and the Native American Indian.* London: Salamander Books Ltd. 1995.

Bankes, George *Native American Woodlands Art in the Manchester Museum Collections.* Paper given at Museum of Mankind, London – Native Art of the North American Woodlands Conference. 26 Feb. Unpublished. 1999.

Berlandier, J. Louis *The Indians of Texas in 1830.* Edited by John C. Ewers. Washington: Smithsonian Institution. 1969.

Birket-Smith, Kaj. Some Ancient Artifacts from the Eastern United States. *Journal de la Société des Americanistes de Paris.* 12–13. 1920.

Bohr, Roland *Plains Indian Archery Gear of the Historic Period.* Seminar Paper. Bismarck: University of North Dakota. 1996.

Bourke, Captain John G. *Remarks. Arrows and Arrow-Makers.* Vol. IV: 71–74. The American Anthropologist. 1891.

Bowers, Alfred W. *Mandan Social and Ceremonial Organization.* Chicago, Illinois: University of Chicago Press. 1950.

Bradley, James H. *Characteristics, habits and customs of the Blackfeet Indians.* Vol. 9. Montana Hist. Soc. Contrib. 1923.

Brasser, Theodore War Clubs. *American Indian Tradition.* Vol. 7. no. 3: 77–83. Alton, Illinois. 1961

Bo'jou, *Neejee!* Ottawa, Ontario: National Museum of Man. 1976.

Early Indian-European Contacts in *Handbook of North American Indians,* Vol. 15 Northeast: 78–88. Washington: Smithsonian Institution. 1978

Brunius, Staffan. Some Comments on Early Swedish Collections from the Northeast in *New Sweden in America*: 150–168. Ed. Hoffecker, Waldron, Williams & Benson. Newark: University of Delaware Press. 1995.

Carver, Jonathan *The Journals of Jonathan Carver: and Related Documents 1766-1770.* Ed. John Parker. St. Paul: Minnesota Historical Society Press. 1976.

Catlin, George *North American Indians*. 2 Vols. Edinburgh: John Grant. 1926

Chandler, Milford G. *The Blacksmith's Shop*: 55–77 in Peterson. 1971.

Coe, Connolly et al *Swords and Hilt Weapons.* London: Weidenfeld and Nicolson. 1989.

Cowdrey, Mike *Spring Boy Rides the Moon: Celestial Patterns in Crow Shield Designs.* Privately published by author. 1995

Culin, Stewart *Games of the North American Indians.* 24th Annual Report of the Bureau of American Ethnology, 1902-03. Washington: Smithsonian Institution. 1907. (Reprint. 1975: New York: Dover Publications).

De Laguna, Frederica. Tlingit in *Handbook of North American Indians,* Vol.7 Northwest Coast:203-228. Ed. Wayne Suttles, Washington: Smithsonian Institution. 1990.

De La Vega, Garcilaso *Florida of the Inca.* Translated by John and Jeannette Varner, Houston: University of Texas Press. 1951

Densmore, Frances *Teton Sioux Music.* Bull.61, Bureau of American Ethnology. Washington: Smithsonian Institution. 1918.

DeVoto, Bernard *Across the Wide Missouri.* London: Eyre and Spottiswoode. 1948.

Dodge, Col. Richard Irving *33 years among our Wild Indians.* New York: Archer House, Inc. 1959.

Ewers, John C. *The Horse in Blackfoot Indian Culture.* Bull.159, Bureau of American Ethnology. Washington: Smithsonian Institution. 1955.

Early White Influence Upon Plains Indian Painting: George Catlin and Carl Bodmer among the Mandan, 1832–34. Vol. 134, No. 7. Misc. Colls. Washington: Smithsonian Institution. 1957.

Blackfoot Indian Pipes and Pipemaking. Anthro. Papers, no. 64. Bureau of American Ethnology. Washington: Smithsonian Institution. 1963.

The White Man's Strongest Medicine. Reprint. St. Louis(?): Bulletin of the Missouri Historical Society. 1967.

Indian Life on the Upper Missouri. Norman: University of Oklahoma Press. 1968.

The Awesome Bear in Plains Indian Art. *American Indian Art.* Vol. 7, No. 3: 36–45. Scottsdale, Arizona. 1982.

Faris and Elmer *Arab Archery.* Princeton: University Press. 1945.

Feest, Christian Essay in *Tradescant Rarities*: 110–115. Ed. Arthur Macgregor. Oxford: Clarendon Press. 1983.

Jacques Le Moyne Minus Four. *European Review of Native American Studies,* 2: 1: 33–38. Vienna. 1988.

Ferg, Alan (ed.) *Western Apache Material Culture:* The Goodwin and Guenther Collections. Tucson: The University of Arizona Press. 1987.

Fletcher, Alice C. and Francis La Flesche *The Omaha Tribe.* 27th Annual Report of the Bureau of American Ethnology. Washington. Smithsonian Institution. 1911.

Galante, Gary. Crow Lance Cases or Sword Scabbards. *American Indian Art.* Vol. 6, No.1.: 64–73. Scottsdale, Arizona. 1980

Garretson, Martin, S. *The American Bison.* New York. 1938.

Gibbs, Peter. The Duke Paul Wilhelm Collection in the British Museum. *American Indian Art.* Vol. 7, no. 3: 52–61. Scottsdale, Arizona. 1982.

Gibson, James R. The Maritime Trade of the North Pacific Coast in *Handbook of North American Indians,* Vol. 4 History of Indian-White Relations: 375–390. Ed. Wilcomb E. Washburn. Washington: Smithsonian Institution 1988.

Goetzmann, William H. and Glyndwr Williams *The Atlas of North American Exploration.* New York: Prentice Hall General Reference. 1992.

Hamilton, T. M. *Native American Bows.* Special publications No. 5. Columbia: Missouri Archaeological Society. 1982.

Hanson, James Austin *Metal Weapons, Tools, and Ornaments of the Teton Dakota Indians.* Lincoln: University of Nebraska Press. 1975.

Heidenreich, Conrad E. Huron in *Handbook of North American Indians,* Vol. 15 Northeast: 368–388. Ed. Bruce G. Trigger. Washington: Smithsonian Institution. 1978.

Hodge, Frederick Webb (ed.) *Handbook of Americans Indians North of Mexico.* 2 Vols. Bull. 30, Bureau of American Ethnology. Washington: Smithsonian Institution 1907–1910. (Reprint. 1965: New York: Rowman and Littlefield Inc.).

Hoebel, E. Adamson Zia Pueblo in *Handbook of North American Indians,* Vol. 9 Southwest: 407–417. Ed. Alfonso Ortiz. Washington: Smithsonian Institution. 1979.

Holm, Bill. The Crow-Nez Perce Otterskin Bowcase-Quiver. *American Indian Art.* Vol. 6, No. 4: 60–70. Scottsdale, Arizona. 1981.

Hothem, Lar *Collecting Indian Knives. Identification and Values.* Alabama: Books

Americana. 1986.

Hotz, Gottfried *Indian Skin Paintings from the American Southwest.* Norman: University of Oklahoma Press. 1970.

Hough, Walter *Arrow Feathering and Pointing in Arrows and Arrow-Makers.* Vol. IV: 60–63. The American Anthropologist. 1891.
Primitive American Armor. Washington: Smithsonian Institution. 1893.

Hulton, Paul *America 1585. The Complete Drawings of John White.* University of North Carolina Press & British Museum Publications. 1984.

Hunt, David C. and Marsha V. Gallagher and William Orr *Karl Bodmer's America.* Joslyn Art Museum & University of Nebraska Press. 1984.

Keyser, James D. *A Shoshonean Origin for the Plains Shield Bearing Warrior Motif.* Vol. 20, No. 69. 1975. Plains Anthropologist.

King, J. C. H. *Smoking Pipes of the North American Indian.* London: British Museum Publications, Limited. 1977.
Thunderbird and Lightning. London: British Museum Publications, Limited. 1982.
Clubs and Tomahawks: the Inversion of Function and Meaning in the 19th Century. Paper given at Museum of Mankind, London – Native Art of the North American Woodlands Conference. 26 Feb. Unpublished. 1999

Klann, Kilian. Die Sammlung indianischer Ethnographica aus Nordamerika des Herzog Friedrich Paul Wilhelm von Württemberg Wyk auf Foehr:Verlag für Amerikanistik. 1999.

Krech, Shepard III *A Victorian Earl in the Arctic: The Travels and Collections of the Fifth Earl of Lonsdale 1888-89.* Seattle: University of Washington Press. 1989.

Kroeber, Alfred L. *The Arapaho.* New York: Bulletin of the American Museum of Natural History. 1902–1907.

Kurz, Rudolph *Journal of Rudolph Friedrich Kurz.* Bull. 115, Bureau of American Ethnology. Ed. J. N. B. Hewitt. Translated by Myrtis Jarrell. Washington: Smithsonian Institution. 1937.

Ladd, Edmund J. *Zuni Social and Political Organization* in *Handbook of North American Indians.* Vol. 9 Southwest: 482–491. Ed. Alfonso Ortiz. Washington: Smithsonian Institution. 1979.

Laubin, Reginald and Gladys *American Indian Archery.* Norman: University of Oklahoma Press. 1980.

Lewis. Meriwether and William Clark *The History of the Lewis and Clark Expedition.* 3 Vols. Ed. Elliott Coues. New York: Francis P. Harper. 1893. (Reprint, Dover Publications Inc., New York).

Lewis, Oscar *The Effects of White Contact upon Blackfoot Culture.* Centennial Anniversary Publication. The American Ethnological Society 1842–1942. Seattle: University of Washington Press. 1942.

Light, D. W. *Tattooing Practices of the Cree Indians.* Occasional Paper No. 6. Calgary: Glenbow-Alberta Institute. 1972.

Lloyd, Christopher and R. C. Anderson (eds.) *A Memoir of James Trevenen.* London: Navy Records Society. 1959.

Loendorf, Lawrence L. and Stuart W. Conner *The Pectol Shields and the Shield-Bearing Warrior Rock Art Motif. Journal of California and Great Basin Anthropology.* Vol. 15, No. 2.: 216–224. 1993.

Lowie, Robert H. *The northern Shoshone.* Anthrop. Paper, Vol. 2. Pt. 2. New York: American Museum of Natural History. 1908.
The Crow Indians. New York: Farrar & Rinehart, Incorporated, on Murray Hill. 1935

Lyford, Carrie A. *Iroquois Crafts.* Lawrence, Kansas: United States Indian Service, Haskell Institute. 1945.

Marquis, TB 1957. *"Wooden Leg; a warrior who fought Custer".* University of Nebraska Press. Lincoln.

McCoy, Ronald *Circles of Power.* Vol. 55, No. 4., in 'Plateau' series. Flagstaff: Museum of Northern Arizona. 1984.
Miniature Shields: James Mooney's Fieldwork among the Kiowa and Kiowa-Apache. American Indian Art. Vol. 20, No. 3: 64–71. Scottsdale, Arizona. 1995.

McKenney, Thomas L. and James Hall *The Indian Tribes of North America.* 3 Vols Edinburgh: John Grant. 1933.

Marquis, Thomas H. *Memoirs of a White Crow Indian.* New York: The Century Company. 1928.

Mason, Otis T. *Arrows and Arrow-Makers.* Vol. IV. The American Anthropologist. 1891.
North American Bows, Arrows, and Quivers. Smithsonian Report (1893): 631–679. Washington: Government Printing Office. 1894.

Maximilian, Prince of Wied *Early Western Travels 1748-1846.* Vol. XXIII. Part II of *Maximilian, Prince of Wied's Travels in the Interior of North America, 1832–1834.* Ed. Reuben Gold Thwaites. Cleveland, Ohio: The Arthur H. Clark Company. 1906.

Mishkin, Bernard. *Rank and Warfare Among the Plains Indians.* Seattle and London: University of Washington Press. 1940.

Morgan, Lewis Henry *The Indian Journals 1859-62.* Ed. Leslie A. White. Ann Arbor: The University of Michigan Press. 1959.

Murray, Alexander Hunter *Journal of the Yukon 1847-48.* Publications of the Canadian Archives No. 4. Ed. L. J. Burpee. Ottawa: Government Printing Bureau. 1910.

Nagy, Imre *A Typology of Cheyenne Shield Designs.* Plains Anthropologist: 39–47.

Owsley, Douglas W. and Richard L. Jantz (eds.) *Skeletal Biology in the Great Plains.* Washington and London: Smithsonian Institution. 1994.

Painter, John W. *American Indian Artifacts: the John Painter Collection.* Cincinnati, Ohio: George Tassian Organization, Inc. 1992.

Parmentier, Richard, J. *The Mythological Triangle: Poseyemu, Montezuma, and Jesus* in the Pueblos in *Handbook of North American Indians,* Vol. 9 Southwest: 609–622. Ed. Alfonso Ortiz. Washington: Smithsonian Institution. 1979.

Peterson, Harold L. *American Knives.* New York: Charles Scribner's Sons. 1957.
American Indian Tomahawks. New York: Museum of the American Indian, Heye Foundation. 1971.

Pfefferkorn, Ignaz. *Pfefferkorn's description of the Province of Sonora.* Ed. Theodore E. Trentlein. Albuquerque: Coronado Cuarto Centennial Publ. Vol. 12. 1949.

Phillips, Ruth B. *Patterns of Power.* Kleinburg, Ontario: The McMichael Canadian Collection. 1984.
Like a Star I Shine in The Spirit Sings. Toronto: McClelland and Stewart. 1987.

Pike, Zebulon M. *An account of expeditions to the sources of the Mississippi, and through the western parts of Louisiana.* Philadelphia. 1810.

Pohrt, Richard A. *Pipe Tomahawks from Michigan and the Great Lakes Area.* Bulletin of the Detroit Institute of Arts. Vol. 62, No. 1: 54–60. Detroit, Michigan. 1986.

Pope, Saxton *A study in Bows and Arrows.* Publications in American Archaeology and Ethnology. University of California. 1923.

Robarchek, Clayton A. Plains Warfare and the Anthropology of War in Owsley and Jantz: 307-316. 1994.

Ross, Marvin C. (Ed.) *The West of Alfred Jacob Miller.* Norman: University of Oklahoma Press. 1968.

Seaver, James E. *The Life of Mary Jemison.* New York: The American Scenic and Historic Preservation Society (Reprint). 1982.

Secoy, Frank Raymond *Changing Military Patterns on the Great Plains.* Seattle: University of Washington Press. 1953.

Smith, DeCost *Indian Experiences.* Caldwell, Idaho: The Caxton Printers Ltd. 1943.

Speck, Frank, G. Notes on the Functional Basis of Decoration and the Feather Technique of the Oglala Sioux. *Indian Notes,* Vol. V, No. 1. New York: Museum of the American Indian. 1928.

Stanislawski, Michael B. Hopi-Tewa in *Handbook of North American Indians,* Vol. 9 Southwest: 587–602. Ed. Alfonso Ortiz. Washington: Smithsonian Institution. 1979.

Stone, G. Cameron *A Glossary of the Construction, Decoration and Use of Arms and Armor.* New York: Jack Brussel. 1934.

Sturtevant, William C. *Iroquois Hieroglyphics.* Paper given at 10th American Indian Workshop. Vienna. 1989.

Sturtevant, William C. And Colin Taylor *The Native Americans.* London: Salamander Books, Ltd. 1991.

Swagerty, William R. Indian Trade in the Trans-Mississippi West to 1870 in *Handbook of North American Indians,* Vol. 4 History of Indian-White Relations: 351–374. Ed. Wilcomb E. Washburn. Washington: Smithsonian Institution. 1988.

Swanton, John R. *Early History of the Creek Indians and Their Neighbours.* Bull 73, Bureau of American Ethnology. Washington: Smithsonian Institution. 1922.

Tate, Marcia *The Atlatl Story.* Tate Enterprises Unlimited, Inc. 1986.

Taylor, Colin *The Warriors of the Plains.* London: The Hamlyn Publishing Group. 1975.

Title essay in *Ho, For the Great West!* The Silver Jubilee Publication. Ed. Barry C. Johnson. London: The English Westerners Society. 1980.

Crow Rendezvous in *Crow Indian Art:* 33–48. Eds. D. & R. Lessard. Mission, South Dakota: Chandler Institute. 1984.

Wakanyan: Symbols of Power and Ritual of the Teton Sioux in *Amerindian Cosmology.* Cosmos 4, Yearbook of the Traditional Cosmology Society. Ed. Don McCaskill. Brandon, Manitoba: The Canadian Journal of Native Studies. 1989.

Native American Myths and Legends. London: Salamander Books Limited. 1994a.

The Plains Indians. London: Salamander Books Limited. 1994b.

Sun'ka Wakan. Sacred Horses of the Plains Indians: Ethos and Regalia. (Bilingual English/German). Wyk auf Foehr: Verlag für Amerikanistik. 1995a.

Myths of the North American Indians. London: Calmann and King Ltd. 1995b.

Catlin's O-kee-pa: Mandan Culture and Ceremonialism. The George Catlin O-keep-pa Manuscript in the British Museum. (Bilingual English/German). Foreword by W. Raymond Wood. Wyk auf Foehr: Verlag für Amerikanistik. 1996.

North American Indians. Avonmouth, Bristol: Parragon. 1997.

Hoka hey! Scalps to coups: the impact of the horse on Plains Indian warfare. Lecture given at the Buffalo Bill Historical Center, Cody, Wyoming. September. 1999. IN PRESS.

Taylor, William E., Jr. And Dale Idiens et al *The Athapaskans: Strangers of the North.* Foreword by Norman Tebble. Ottawa: National Museum of Man and Edinburgh: Royal Scottish Museum. 1974.

Teit, James A. *The Salishan Tribes of the Western Plateaus.* 45th Annual Report of the Bureau of American Ethnology. Ed. Franz Boas. Washington: Government Printing Office. 1930.

Turner, Geoffrey *Indians of North America.* Poole, Dorset: Blandford Press. 1979.

Underhill, Ruth *Indians of the Pacific Northwest.* Washington: Bureau of Indian Affairs, Branch of Education. 1945.

Utley, Robert M. *The Lance and The Shield: The Life and Times of Sitting Bull.* New York: Ballantine Books. 1993.

Vennum, Thomas Jr. *American Indian Lacrosse: Little Brother of War.* Washington and London: Smithsonian Institution Press. 1994.

Wallace, Ernest and E. Adamson Hoebel *The Comanches: Lords of the South Plains.* Norman: University of Oklahoma Press. 1952.

Wildschut, William and John C. Ewers *Crow Indian Beadwork.* New York: Museum of the American Indian. 1959.

Wildschut, William *Crow Indian Medicine Bundles.* Ed. John C. Ewers. New York: Museum of the American Indian. 1960.

Wilson, Thomas *Arrow Wounds.* N.S.3., American Anthropologist. 1901.

Wissler, Clark. *Decorative Art of the Sioux Indians.* Vol. XVIII. New York: American Museum of Natural History. 1904.

Some Protective Designs of the Dakota. Vol. I, Part II. New York: American Museum of Natural History. 1907.

Material Culture of the Blackfoot Indians. Vol. V. New York: American Museum of Natural History. 1910.

Social Organization and Ritualistic Ceremonies of the Blackfoot Indians. Vol. VII, Part I. New York: American Museum of Natural History. 1912.

Woodward, Arthur The Metal Tomahawk: Its Evolution and Distribution in North America in *The Bulletin of the Fort Ticonderoga Museum,* 3,3. 1946.

Indian Trade Goods. Portland: Oregon Archaeological Society. 1965.

Wright, Barton *Pueblo Shields.* Flagstaff, Arizona: Northland Press. 1976.

Pueblo Shields. *American Indian Art.* Vol. 17, No. 2: 44-51. Scottsdale, Arizona. 1992.

Index

Picture Credits